# MEMORIES OF A
# WARTIME
# CHILDHOOD
# IN LONDON

# MEMORIES OF A
# WARTIME
# CHILDHOOD
# IN LONDON

## DOUGLAS MODEL

The
History
Press

This book is dedicated to everyone who has been harmed by war.

Some names, details and locations have been changed to protect privacy. Every reasonable care has been taken to avoid copyright infringements, and any valid issues that may arise will be corrected in subsequent editions.

*Front cover image:* CBW/Alamy Stock Photo.

First published 2022

The History Press
97 St George's Place, Cheltenham,
Gloucestershire, GL50 3QB
www.thehistorypress.co.uk

British Library Cataloguing in Publication Data.
A catalogue record for this book is available from the British Library.

ISBN 978 0 7509 9962 5

Typesetting and origination by The History Press
Printed and bound in Great Britain by TJ Books Limited, Padstow, Cornwall.

MIX
Paper from
responsible sources
FSC® C013056

Trees for LYfe

# CONTENTS

# 1

# IN THE BEGINNING

The day of 3 September 1939 was a quiet one, a typical Sunday of that era when shops were not allowed to open and most people spent the morning in church, then went home to a roast lunch, and spent the afternoon reading the papers, taking a walk, or having a nap.

The world at that time was still recovering from the Great Depression and life was very different to life today. There were very few restaurants and few people ate out. Few homes had telephones, and fewer still had central heating. There were no jet aeroplanes, smartphones, internet or TV, no McDonald's, Burger King or Hilton Hotels. But despite the lack of these things that most people today take for granted and probably think are essential, the majority of people in Britain in 1939 led happy and stable lives.

Happiness, I now realise after a long life, depends not so much on possessions and technology, as on loving and being loved, being healthy – or at least healthy enough to do the things you wish to do – having good friends, having hope, and – if you are lucky enough – having a job and enough money to enjoy yourself and do more than just get by.

The world at that time was very different in other ways to the world of today. The average weekly wage for a man was between £3 and £5, but prices were correspondingly low. A loaf of bread cost 4d (2p in today's money), a pint of milk 3d (1½p), an ordinary semi-detached house in south-east England between £500 and £600 (about £840 in London), and a brand-new family car about £160 to £200. Even so, few people could afford a car. In total, there were about 2 million vehicles on the road in 1939, compared with 40 million today. Few people had travelled abroad. Instead, most people took holidays in Britain, travelling by train to places such as Blackpool, Scarborough, Devon, Cornwall – or for the more energetic, the Lake District, the Peak District or the Highlands of Scotland. But although these things were the accepted norms of the time, that particular Sunday, 3 September 1939, was far from normal, as it was the day when the Second World War broke out, and the peaceful world into which I had been born and brought up changed forever.

I was 6 years old at the time and had just learnt to tie my own shoelaces. On that particular morning, I was with my parents and 4-year-old brother Richard in the drawing room of the flat in which we lived over the shop my mother and father owned in Wembley, a suburb of north-west London. We had just listened on the radio to the prime minister, Mr Neville Chamberlain, tell the nation that regretfully, once again, just twenty years after the slaughter of the First World War, in which millions of people had been killed, we were again at war with Germany. My parents were stunned by the news, and were quietly trying to absorb its implications, and the realisation that the period of indecision that had preceded the declaration was over and that the shooting war was about to begin, when suddenly a whistle sounded in the street outside. Following my mother, or Mum as I called her, I walked over to the window and watched as she pulled back the net curtain to reveal a man on a bicycle gesticulating wildly with his free arm as he cycled along the road. He was wearing a tin helmet on his head, and was obviously trying to attract attention.

'What on earth's the matter with him? Is he mad?' Mum asked, as I stood watching beside her.

Later, we learnt that the man was an air-raid warden, and that as the air-raid sirens that had been installed were not yet operational in the area in which we lived, he was doing his best to warn us that an air raid was about to take place. Fortunately, it proved to be a false alarm and nothing untoward happened. It was the beginning of what became known as the Phoney War, during which, for the first eight months of the war, Britain was not involved in any fighting on land, although at sea both we and the Germans lost several ships. These included the British liner *Athenia*, which was torpedoed by a German U-boat with the loss of 112 lives just a few hours after the declaration of war, and the battleship HMS *Royal Oak*, torpedoed with the loss of 800 lives while she was at anchor in Scapa Flow, a deep-water so-called safe haven off the north of Scotland.

★★★

The events of 3 September 1939 are not my earliest memory by any means. That honour belongs to a hiking holiday my parents took me on in 1934, walking along the River Rhine in Germany. I was aged almost 2 at the time, and my brother Richard had not yet been born. I have just one memory of the holiday, and that is of being carried down a sloping gangway into the dark interior of a ship that I know now was the ferry that was to carry us across the English Channel to the Continent. Throughout the holiday, Dad carried me on his back in a carry chair, while Mum carried our clothes in a rucksack. When I was older, Mum told me that to attract Dad's attention while sitting on his back, I would say, 'Hey, Joe, look over there,' and pull his ear in the direction in which I wished him to look.

The author aged 2½.

In total, Mum and Dad walked about 60 miles along the Rhine. In many places they saw evidence of German rearming. In some of the bed-and-breakfast homes in which we stayed, they found military uniforms in the wardrobes, and an army rifle in one. Photographs of Hitler hung in some of the homes and in most official buildings. As they walked along the Rhine, ordinary Germans greeted them with a raised arm and the words '*Heil Hitler*'. In one small town, Dad had to hurry Mum out of a bank in which they were changing money, when in faltering German, while looking up at a photo of Hitler, Mum said, 'The Führer is a *Schweinehund*'.

When we got back from Germany, Mum found a teaspoon bearing the inscription 'Belishor Hof Hotel Köln' in the rucksack she had carried throughout the holiday. As neither she nor Dad had taken the spoon, they assumed that I had placed it in the rucksack. Later, when I was aged about 6, I claimed it as my own, and would not use any other teaspoon. If I could not find it, I searched the kitchen for it and, if still I could not find it, only then would I grudgingly settle for another.

***

My next early memory is of a party my parents threw about eighteen months or so after we returned from Germany. The occasion was to celebrate the birth of Richard. At that time we still lived in a small three-up, two-down semi-detached house about half a mile behind the shop. It was in the sort of side street in which the lives of the lower middle classes were played out behind closed doors. I remember it well: the stale, still air in homes in which windows were hardly ever opened, and the feeling that nothing of much significance ever happened, which may or may not have been true. The lives of many people who lived in that type of house were happy, with the man of the house going out to work during the week and his wife staying at home to bring up the family.

I was aged nearly 3 at the time and remember standing at the foot of the stairs in the hall of our house, and because I was so small, seeing that my line of vision was in the same straight line as the leading edges of the carpeted wooden steps that led up to the floor above. I also remember looking up at the forest of adults standing around me with glasses in their hands, swaying over me like trees in the wind. Several years later, when I was aged about 10, my parents told me that after the party I drained as many empty glasses as I could find and afterwards lapsed into an alcoholic stupor. At first, I sang and gurgled in baby fashion, then I settled down and slept for eighteen hours. As a result, when appropriate, in the right company, I like to boast that I was drunk for the first time at the age of 2½.

My next memory of that time is of Richard being washed in a tin bath on the floor of the room that passed for our living room. He must have been around 6 months. In that memory, I see him as a small baby lying back in Mum's hand, his lower half immersed in soapy water, his upper abdomen, chest and head supported by Mum's hand and arm.

I have other memories of that time, and know that they relate to the period before I was 4 because we moved to the shop when I was that age. Before we moved, the people in the house next door were a couple named Bob

Mum, aged 50.                    Dad, aged 51.

and Jenny Murison. Bob was a solicitor, and their house was detached and much larger than ours. Several years later, Bob spent some time in a psychiatric hospital as a result of depression brought on by guilt and the fear of being imprisoned for falsifying his company's tax returns.

The Murisons had a large black Labrador dog, and I remember standing under their kitchen table with his black face and eyes level with mine, and his tongue lolling out as he panted and patiently indulged me while I tried to pat him.

The house attached to the other side of our home was a mirror image of our house, in which a family named the Boltings lived. I used to play with Graham, their son, and Mum used to talk to Mrs Bolting over the back garden fence, typically when they were hanging out their washing on Monday mornings – the morning during which almost every housewife in Britain washed and hung out her family's laundry. Mr Bolting was a bank manager, and they were considerably better off than we were. Many years later Graham went to Berkhamsted, one of England's so-called public schools, which are private and very expensive, and not really public at all.

Another thing I remember of the time before we moved to the shop was my father finding a blackbird with a broken wing in the garden at the back of the house. I was almost 4 at the time, and remember that Dad brought the bird into the house and placed it on a mat on the floor of our living room – we used the drawing room only on Sundays – and tried to feed it bits of bread soaked in whisky until eventually a tall man wearing a chauffeur's-type cap, and what I imagine was an RSPCA uniform, came and took the bird away in a basket.

My next early memory is of a man shouting, 'Anything for the rag-and-bone man?' Dressed in down-at-heel, grubby, black clothes, and seated on a cart drawn by a tired-looking horse, he drove passed our house and passed the house on the opposite side of the road in which the famous bandleader Victor Sylvester lived.

One of my happiest memories of that time before the war, when the world seemed so peaceful and settled, was of a man wearing a big red Bakelite cat's head over his head, as he collected money for charity. Even now, more than eighty years later, I remember the excitement I felt at his appearance. Mum knew the time and day of the month that he came, and would open the front door for me, so that I could stand, watching and waiting for him. When he appeared, I would run out to the front garden gate, shouting 'Cats, cats!' and give him the couple of coppers that Mum had given me for the purpose.

★★★

In 1937, when I was aged 4, my parents took me to see the newly built corner shop and the flat above it that was to be our new home. Neither the shop nor the flat had been occupied before, and the bricks of its outside walls and the red tiles high up on its sloping roof were new and much brighter and cleaner-looking than those of the much older next-door shop onto which it abutted.

Mum and Dad with the author, aged 2½.

'How would you like to live here?' Dad asked, bending over me, as we stood looking up at the building from its unpaved, bare earth back yard.

I must have answered affirmatively, as we moved in shortly afterwards.

***

One of my abiding memories of that time, when I was still only 4, is of sitting without any clothes on, on the draining board in the kitchen of the flat, with my feet in the large porcelain kitchen sink, and the hot and cold water taps in front of me. On the wall behind me, our gas-burning Ascot Geyser was heating the water with which Mum was about to wash me. In her right hand was a large white flannel soaked with soap.

'First I'll do your front and back,' she said, tickling my tummy and making me laugh.

I watched, as gently she rubbed first my front and then my back with the soapy flannel.

When she had finished washing me, she draped a large, dry towel over my back, kissed the back of my neck, and gently dried me. As she was doing so, her face came close to mine, and a warm glow filled me and I felt very loved.

'Was that nice?' she asked, when she had finished.

She asked me to stand up, and said, 'Now, darling, I'll do your bottom and winkle.'

When they were done, she asked me to climb down to the floor. I was already too heavy for her to lift so, guided by her, I climbed out of the sink and onto a kitchen stool that had been placed close by, and clambered down onto the floor. When she was sure I was safe, she turned to

16

Richard, who was still only 2, and was sitting on the floor wearing a nappy, and said, 'Now, Richard, darling. It's your turn to be made a nice clean boy like your big brother.'

From the kitchen floor on which he was sitting, Richard reached up his arms towards her, and laughed, as she bent down and put her hands round his little chest, and lifted him up.

***

Before she married, Mum had managed a grocery shop on behalf of an older brother named Alexander, or Sander as he was known in the family, and it was her ambition to open a ladies' clothes shop in her own right in Wembley.

The shop had to be fitted out before it could be opened. Dad did that. As jobs had been difficult to get when he was young during the Great Depression, he had reluctantly trained to be a ladies' hairdresser, but at heart and by instinct he was a one-man building firm, who could lay bricks and make furniture almost as well as a tradesman. Without having had any formal training, he could plumb and wire a house. So, it wasn't any surprise that he fitted out the shop himself with me watching happily beside him as he painted throughout, fitted lights, and built sliding wooden doors behind the windows, separating them from the main part of the shop.

Mum and Dad slept in the bedroom at the front of the flat, and Richard and I in the one at the back. Dad decorated our bedroom with wallpaper chosen specially for us as boys, with a repeat pattern of monkeys climbing palm trees and eating bananas.

Our home in 1960.

The shop in 2021.

Mum was musical and had played the violin since child-hood. She also had a fine singing voice. When we were settled in the flat, she often came into our bedroom at bedtime and sung us to sleep. I can see her now, standing by Richard's bed in the half-light created by the drawn curtains, with a large dark wardrobe and the monkey pattern wallpaper behind her, looking down at us as we lay safely under the bedcovers, watching her as she sang her own version of the song 'Ma Curly Headed Baby' that was as follows:

Tulla, lulla, lulla, lulla, bye, bye
Does you want the moon to play with
Or the stars to run away with
Oh, tulla, lulla, lulla, lulla bye.[*]

Listening, we felt very safe and secure, and in next to no time were fast asleep.

At other times, as we lay in our little cribs, watching her, Mum played us to sleep with her violin.

★★★

Shortly after moving to the flat, Mum and Dad became friends with neighbours living in a large, detached house in the side road on the side of the shop. The Ferrises, as we called Mr and Mrs Ferris, had a large garden with a pond containing water lilies and a bridge over which I liked to run. Richard and I played in the Ferrises' garden with their daughter Rita, who now lives in New Zealand, but

[*]  Adapted from the original song by George H. Clutson.

with whom I still keep in touch, as old friends are the best friends. Rita had a brown wigwam tent with Red Indian signs painted on it in yellow and white, and the three of us played cowboys and Indians in it for hours, only stopping when we were called for meals.

Mrs Ferris made the best fruitcake I have ever tasted, although she was mean with it and only served it in tiny slices. Meanwhile, whenever Mum (poor woman) made cakes, Richard and I scraped and ate the cake mix from the saucepan in which she had mixed it and, along with Dad, sat round the oven and wolfed down the cakes as fast as they were produced.

Mrs Ferris grew grapes in a south-facing conservatory that Richard and I were rarely allowed in. She was something of a stickler for manners, but had no experience of boys and looked upon Richard and me as wild. Whenever she could, tried to improve our behaviour and manners. One day, she caught us having a pee down a drain at the back of the shop. She was not amused, although I am pleased to say that, having expressed her displeasure, she forgave us, and many years later, when I was emerging from the chrysalis-like state of childhood and was becoming aware of the world around me, thirsting for knowledge in the first blossoming of adulthood, she was the person to whom I turned for information about the arts and which books I should read.

★★★

When in 1938 I was aged 5, an exciting event occurred: I started school. The school in question was Barham School, a government primary school situated in a quiet suburban residential area of semi-detached houses about half a mile from our home above the shop. Mum took me there on the first few occasions; subsequently, I walked there and back on my own. I liked school. If I had been good at home, before I set out Mum gave me a couple of pence to spend at the end of the day on buying an ice lolly from a man outside the school selling Wall's ice creams that he took from a wooden freezer box mounted on a tricycle.

The school was a good one. The headmistress was a kindly, thin middle-aged lady named Miss Hill, whose dark hair, in keeping with the fashion of the day, was tightly curled against her head. I liked Miss Hill; she was kind to me. My class teacher was also kind. She was a plump, middle-aged, mumsy lady named Miss Swan. As both she and Miss Hill were much taller than me, I remember them looking down at me as they spoke to me. Miss Swan encouraged me, and I enjoyed her class. In it I learnt to read simple words like 'wood' and 'ship' and tried to copy words from the blackboard, and from a special copybook that had sentences in copperplate writing on one line that I tried to copy on the line below. The school was well equipped and had a large room in which we learnt about everyday tasks through play. There was a mock-up road where, along with friends I had made in class, I practised looking left, then right, then left again before crossing the road at a mock crossing complete with mock Belisha beacons, similar to the flashing beacons at modern pedestrian crossings. There was also a mock kitchen with worktops at an appropriate height at which we played at weighing food and cooking, and a mock-up shop, where we learnt to use money, either as shopkeeper or as customer. The playground at the back of the school was big and partly tarred and partly grassed. At its back were several large oak trees that separated it from the Piccadilly line, along which trains passed one way or the other every few minutes. In the autumn, the trees were a great source of acorns that we swapped with one another.

I fell in love for the first time in that playground. The subject of my affections was all of 5 years old, the same age as me. Her name was Jennifer Gray, and my love for her was shy and tinged with pain borne of a feeling that she might reject me. To help overcome my apprehension and win her to my cause, one day I bought her a thruppenny paper bag of coconut candy flakes from Mr Hill, an elderly man who ran a sweetshop called The Chocolate Box in the parade of shops in which we lived. To get enough money to pay for the candy flakes, I saved my ice lolly money for a couple of days.

Mr Hill and his wife watched for people coming into their shop from armchairs placed near the door of a comfortably furnished sitting room at the back of the shop. On seeing me enter, Mr Hill rose and walked slowly towards me. On his feet were bedroom slippers.

'Umm,' he said suspiciously, looking down and fixing me through his glasses when I asked him for the sweets. 'Are you sure you've got enough money, sonny?'

'Umm' summed him up perfectly, as he looked perpetually glum, never smiled and behaved as if he had the weight of the world upon his shoulders.

I showed him the thruppence I was holding in my clenched fist, and watched as he took a large jar from a shelf on the wall behind him and slowly emptied a generous helping of its contents into a small white paper bag he had placed on the scales in front of him.

The following day I gave the sweets to Jennifer, who smiled and accepted them gracefully without comment. The day after that, while we were running together in the playground during a break from school, I blurted out, 'I love you, Jennifer!' Jennifer was flushed and breathless from running and flushed even more and her mouth stretched up towards her ears in a great big smile, but she said nothing, and I was left not knowing what she felt, and my pain was greater than ever.

# 2

# PREPARING
# FOR WAR

**B**ritain began preparing for the possibility of war several years before it actually occurred. Perhaps because of our holiday in Germany, Dad suspected that there was going to be a war. As he had a large hernia in his groin, he was not eligible for the armed services; instead, he signed up to be a policeman in the event of hostilities. When they started, he was called up and became War Reserve 692, a full-time policeman, patrolling the streets and preventing and reporting crime, and later patrolling the town during bombing raids and guarding bombed-out buildings and unexploded bombs.

About eighteen months after we moved into the flat, while the country was still at peace, we were issued with gas masks. I hated mine. Some children were lucky enough to get one that had a Mickey Mouse face with a loose rubber extension on its front that stuck out and served as a nose. Mine, by contrast, was a bog-standard, ordinary

Standard-issue gas mask. (The Print Collector/Alamy)

black one with a metal snout at its end. It encompassed my face and was so tight that it pressed into my skin and made me feel shut in and I could not talk at all, or breathe or see properly through its Perspex eyepiece. However, I could amuse myself with it by breathing in hard enough to suck most of the air out of it and bring its metal snout up against my nose with a thump.

Richard was issued with a gas mask for a baby by mistake. It was huge and looked like a deep-sea diver's helmet into which the baby was put. It was meant for a child aged up to about 2, and as by then Richard was big for a boy aged 3, Mum exchanged it for one like mine.

A few months later, Dad decided to build an air-raid shelter for us on a spare piece of land that my parents owned behind the shop. I remember the man who assisted him with building it. Paddy was a kind, blue-eyed Irishman with yellow-blond hair and a broad Irish brogue. He wore a washed-out old blue shirt, and allowed me to help him by pouring water onto the mixture of sand and cement that was to become concrete. The shelter was almost entirely underground and had a curved, corrugated iron roof covered by 6in or more of concrete, and was so strong that it would have withstood all but a direct hit. Building it wasn't entirely without problems. One afternoon, part of a wall started to fall in while the concrete was still wet. Dad and Paddy saved the situation by pushing it back with wooden boards, but the shelter ended up smaller inside than intended. Months later, it rocked as bombs fell nearby, but it did not so much as crack.

When neighbours looked over the fence and saw the shelter being built, they laughed as they passed by, and said, 'Old Model's got the wind up. It will be alright. There isn't going to be any war.' But they changed their minds, and were pleased to come into the shelter when the bombing began.

While these preparations for war were going on, our lives proceeded in a peaceful way. Dad, who at that time was aged 31, owned a Morris 7, a tiny car like a box on wheels, rolling along on spindly wheels at 30–40mph. Its back was tucked in like the back of an old-fashioned horse-drawn carriage. At a guess, I would say its maximum speed was no more than about 60mph. Inside, the front two seats of the car were roomy enough, but there was precious little room in the back, although that didn't bother small people such as Richard and me, as our thin, childlike legs required little room.

The main attractions of the car for Richard and me were the large silver headlights on either side of its bonnet, and a glass gauge on the top of the bonnet from which, as you sat in your seat, you could read the temperature of the water in the radiator. To be able to read the water temperature was important, as car radiators of that time were liable to boil over and were prone to leaking, so they could run dry in a matter of minutes, causing the engine to overheat and the car to stop.

We boys loved going out in the car as it heralded a few hours of adventure, and its confined space gave us a feeling of intimacy and that we had Mum and Dad to ourselves.

We usually argued about which side of the car we wanted to sit in, and if we started to push and shove one another, Dad would intervene and say, 'Get in and don't argue, or I'll give you both something to think about!'

We knew the rules, and when that happened, we knew we had to get in as quickly as possible and settle down and be quiet.

As the car trundled along, we would ask Mum to sing to us.

'Mum, sing "Spaniards",' we would shout to her from our seats in the back, or 'Mum, sing "In Eleven More Months and Ten More Days".'

The Spaniard we were referring to was in the song 'The Spaniard that Blighted My Life', made famous by Al Jolson and Bing Crosby. The words Mum sang to its tune are as follows:

List to me whilst I tell you of the Spaniard who blighted my life
List to me whilst I tell you of the man who stole my future wife

28

It was at the bull fight that I met him, I was watching his
daring display
Then whilst I went out for some nuts and a paper
The dirty dog stole her away
Ah, yes, Ah yes, but I swore I would have my revenge
So, when I meet Alfonso, the Spaniard, the blighter I will
kill, tiddly, aye, tye, tye, tye
He shall die. He shall die. He shall die, tiddly, aye, tye, tye,
tye, tye, tye, tye
For I'll raise a bunion on his Spanish onion when I catch
him bending tonight!*

'In Eleven More Months ...' was written by Fred Hall and
Arthur Fields. I remember two lines as follows:

In eleven more months and ten more days I'll be out of
the calaboose.
In eleven more months and ten more days they're going
to turn me loose.

A few months before the war, Dad sold the Morris 7 and
bought a brand-new fawn Austin 12 for about £200. Its
registration number was BMX 375, which I remember
to this day – although I cannot remember the registration numbers of most of the cars I subsequently owned
myself. The Austin was larger and more luxurious than
the Morris, and had blinds in the windows at the back
that the driver could raise or lower from the driving
seat by pulling on a cord beside his head. It also had a
useful luggage net fixed to the inside of the roof in front

* Adapted from the original song by Billy Merson.

of the heads of passengers in the back seats. Like the Morris, it had shiny silver headlights. If I stared at their shiny surface, my face was reflected back in miniature, and if I stuck my tongue out, it appeared bigger than my face. The car had running boards beneath its doors, and Richard and I stepped onto them to get into the car. We also liked to stand on the running boards when the car was parked outside the garage, pretending we were Chicago gangsters hanging on to the outside of the car and using our first two fingers as make-believe guns. Other things I liked about that car were that it had real leather seats and a boot at its back that stuck out behind it a little, instead of a tucked in boot like the Morris 7 and other old-fashioned cars.

★★★

My last memory of that time before the war when the world was still at peace was going by car with Mum, Dad and Richard to visit a battleship moored alongside a quay in Portsmouth Harbour on the south coast of England. I remember standing on its foredeck, with its huge guns pointing forwards above me, and a few minutes later, visiting the ship's bakery, which opened onto the outside deck. The baker was standing in front of the bakery and was wearing a tall chef's white hat and a white apron over his baker's uniform. He joked with Dad, and teasingly offered me a loaf of bread, from which at first I withdrew. Then, extending my arms in a gesture of wanting it, I reached out for it, although I don't remember whether I was given it.

I cannot be certain how real my next memory of that day is, or whether perhaps it is a figment of my imagination, but in my mind's eye, I see myself aged 6 standing inside one of the ship's huge gun turrets and being shown how the shells were loaded.

# 3

# THE PHONEY WAR

On 1 September 1939 – two days before war was declared – the government imposed a night-time blackout. All windows and doors had to be covered from dusk to dawn to prevent the escape of any light that might be seen by and aid enemy aircraft. Mum bought blackout material and made curtains for each of our windows. Air-raid wardens enforced the blackout, and I remember one knocking at our front door one evening to inform Mum and Dad that a chink of light was showing from the edge of our kitchen window.

'Just a warning this time, Sir. But don't let it happen again,' the warden said to Dad, who was at home and off duty at the time. 'We don't want to help Jerry, do we?'

In anticipation of heavy bombing, many thousands of children were evacuated from their homes in the cities and taken to new homes in the countryside, or sent by ship to families in Canada and the United States, but Richard and I were not among them. Mum and Dad decided that we should remain with them in Wembley.

So that I should be able to get home quickly in the event of continuous bombing, I was taken away from Barham School and sent to a small private school in a big old house about 200 yards from our home. Wembley House School had fewer facilities than Barham School, but the teaching was good and it served me well. The literature and history classes in particular were excellent. Long, detailed classics were reduced to thin, soft-covered books of about forty or fifty pages specially tailored to our young age. I loved the story of *Masterman Ready*, a classic tale about an eighteenth-century family who, along with an old sailor, were shipwrecked on a tropical island. As the family included children, I was able to identify with them, and remember the story to this day. There was also the shortened version of Homer's *Odyssey*, and we read how it took ten years for the Greek victors from Troy to get back to their homes in Greece. Among the stories from the *Odyssey* that I remember are the tales of Circe, a beautiful temptress who lured the Greeks onto her island and turned a number of them into pigs; Polyphemus, a frightening one-eyed giant who lived in a cave and tried to kill and eat the Greeks; and the beautiful Sirens, who tried to lure them onto the rocks of their island by singing and playing magical music to them as their ship sailed past. In history, I imagined myself to be the Roman hero Horatio who, sword in hand, saved Rome from the invading Etruscans by holding them at bay on a narrow wooden bridge traversing the River Tiber. On another day, I thrilled to the story of the sacred geese who saved Rome from the invading Gauls. As I understood it, the Romans had been routed and had taken refuge on top of a steep hill known as the Capitoline Hill. While they were asleep one night, the Gauls started to climb the hill, and in doing so disturbed the sacred geese, whose honking and cackling roused the Romans and enabled them to defend themselves.

The fees at Wembley House School were three guineas or £3.30 per term to start with, increasing to £5 after I had been there a year or two. Mrs Moore, the principal, was a business-like, Oxford-educated lady with short black hair that bounced up and down as she hurried about. She was assisted by several teachers, all of whom were women, except for a part-time elderly male teacher named Mr Jarratt, whose main role, so far as I could ascertain, was to give me three across the hand or backside with a cane on the few occasions that, apparently, I warranted it.

Most of the children in the school were well-behaved little paragons, but there were exceptions. A girl named Doreen would take down her pants in the doorway of the girls' toilet to any boy who cared to pay her a thruppence. I didn't pay her, but muscled in on a boy who had, although all I saw were the cheeks of her bare, white bottom and was no wiser about female anatomy than I had been before. But I was embarrassed and could only conclude that Doreen was a very silly girl.

Shortly after I moved to Wembley House School, the government instructed parents to send a box, or preferably a tin, of 'iron rations' to their child's school in case severe bombing prevented the child from being able to get home. The parents of most children at the school gave them tins containing such desirables as a packet or two of biscuits, some crisps, a bar of chocolate, and other non-perishable foods. Some boxes were quite elaborate and made me jealous, as Mum and Dad said that I didn't need one because I would always be able to run home in the event of a serious air raid.

On several occasions we practised what we should do if we were bombed and gassed while at school. On hearing the bell that signalled the practice, we gathered up our gas masks from beside our desks and made our way as quickly and as silently as possible to a large room at the back of the house where we put on our gas masks for perhaps three or four minutes. We hoped to be allowed to eat our iron rations, although, as I didn't have any, I was left feeling embarrassed and different to the other children.

★★★

Despite having been at war for almost three months, Christmas 1939 was almost normal, although because of the blackout there were no Christmas lights and only dull lighting in the streets. Richard and I woke up at about two o'clock in the morning and got out of bed, closed our bedroom door very quietly, so as not to wake Mum and Dad, turned on the light and, with giggles of delight, found the pillowcases in which Dad, standing in for Santa Claus, had placed our presents at the foot of our beds.

As I was opening my pillowcase, I heard Richard tearing open a package.

'Look, I've got snakes and ladders!' he exclaimed.

'And I've got Monopoly,' I replied.

Each of us had been given a stocking containing some wartime luxuries that had been made available specially for children, such as a bar of chocolate and an orange, and a few chocolate pennies wrapped in silver paper.

A sound outside our bedroom caused us to stop what we were doing and listen.

'Quick! It's Dad! Turn out the light and get into bed!'

Before we could turn out the light, Dad opened the door and came in, wearing striped pyjamas.

'Happy Christmas! There's good boys,' he said. 'You've had a good look. Now get back into bed, and leave it till morning.'

He waited until we had settled, then turned out the light and shut the door.

'Shall we get up again?' Richard asked into the darkness when he was certain that Dad was once again in bed. 'I want to see more of my presents.'

'Wait a bit. Then we'll get up and have another look,' I replied.

First thing on Christmas morning, Dad lit a coal fire in the drawing room – the room that we used only on Sundays, high days and holidays. For the other six days of the week it was left unused. It was cold. Double glazing had been invented only a few years previously, but was not yet used in Britain, and as a consequence the wind whistled through ill-fitting windows. Very few homes had central heating, and in the winter it was particularly cold in the flat first thing in the morning. Often, I saw ice on the inside of our bedroom window and on the windows in the bathroom. In an attempt to keep out draughts, Dad had fitted a thick curtain behind the front door and behind the two doors that led into the drawing room. To help exclude draughts entering beneath doors, we placed sausage-shaped draught excluders against the bottom of them. But still the draughts came in, and still the flat was cold.

Coal for the fire was kept in a small coal cellar beneath the stairs leading up to the flat. Getting coal from it and taking it up to the drawing room was one of the jobs Richard and I were expected to do. When the cellar was empty, Dad shovelled up the dust in the bottom of it and made coal bricks from it, using a small rectangular wooden frame he had made for the purpose.

Lighting a fire was quite a business. First, Dad looked for any cinders that remained from the last occasion on which the fire had been lit. Fortunately, that Christmas morning there weren't any. If there had been, he would have had to shovel them out, which would have created a lot of dust. The fire then had to be made up with old newspaper, firewood and coal, placed on top of one another in that order.

When that was done, I asked Dad if I might light the fire. He held a box of matches while I struck a match against it and applied it to the paper. Instantly, the paper burst into flame. To encourage the fire, Dad held a double sheet of newspaper across the front of the fireplace, causing an upward rush of air from beneath the grate that acted like a fan, resulting in the flames becoming larger and the wood, and eventually the coal, catching fire. In half an hour, the part of the room close to the fire was warm, but the further parts were still cold.

Christmas lunch that day was at the mahogany table in the front room, and consisted of roast turkey and all the trimmings. Richard and I argued over who was to have a leg of the bird, but Dad settled the argument by telling us to be good boys and pipe down and giving each of us part of a leg. But the day was different for families with members working away from home or fighting abroad, and for children who had been evacuated and were too far away to return home for the festivities.

At just before three o'clock, as the light was fading from the wintery world outside, we moved to the kitchen to listen to the king give his traditional speech over the radio. Because of the war, what he said that day was particularly significant as it bound the nation together. It was one of the highlights of that Christmas and subsequent Christmases throughout the war, and indeed for the rest of my life (although, of course, the speeches have been delivered by Queen Elizabeth II since 1952). Sitting round the radio, we heard the king's voice come stuttering across the ether. He sounded distant, as if he was a long way away, as broadcasting was still in its infancy at that time: the BBC was still less than twenty years old and radios were relatively primitive. Most radios consisted of a large, polished wooden case in which, among other things, were several glass valves that frequently 'blew' and had to be replaced.

The king greeted the empire and all its citizens, but his stutter was so severe, poor man, that it was painful to listen to him. Long gaps punctuated his words, each of which sounded as if it had been formed in pain. Dad had given each of the family, including Richard and me, a small glass of port, and after the speech, while we were still sitting round the radio, Dad said, 'Raise your glasses! Here's to us all, and here's to everyone on Earth. And here's to the end of the war. Let's hope peace comes soon to the world.'

★★★

In January 1940, when we had been at war for almost five months, the seriousness of our situation began to be evident. Ration books were issued, and within a few months our weekly ration of food amounted to:

1 egg
8oz sugar
Meat to a value of 1s 2d (approximately $£\frac{1}{18}$)
4 rashers of bacon
2oz cheese
2oz butter
4oz margarine
3oz sweets
2oz tea
1lb jam every two months
3 pints milk

Bread and vegetables were not rationed and were freely available. Coffee was available, but was mixed with chicory to make it go further.

Later in the war, as U-boats sank more and more Allied ships bringing supplies to Britain, food became scarcer and rationing was extended to include many more foods, including rice, breakfast cereals, biscuits, tinned tomatoes and dried fruit.

Rations didn't bother Richard and me as we were happy to fill up on bread and dripping, made tasty with salt and pepper. Dripping was beef fat collected from the roasting pan that was allowed to cool and solidify. It tasted wonderful when spread on bread, and frequently after lunch we ate a slice of bread spread thick with it. Soap was rationed later in the war, which again, as we were boys with an aversion to soap and water, was sheer heaven for Richard and me.

Rationing had its positive effects. Obesity became uncommon and for the first time, poor people received a proper diet and a fair share of the nation's food. As a result, vitamin deficiency diseases such as rickets, which was relatively common among the poor before the war, all but disappeared.

Under the slogan 'Dig for Victory' people were encouraged to grow food in their gardens and on their allotments to help increase the supply of food. Richard and I both helped the programme. Mum gave each of us a small patch of one of her flower beds in which we grew lettuces, spring onions and carrots that the family subsequently ate, although Richard didn't produce much as he kept pulling up his plants to see how they were growing. Dad grew masses of tomatoes on the sun-exposed convex layer of earth covering our air-raid shelter.

For most of the war, the poster overleaf, exhorting the population to grow food, embellished the wall of the shop opposite our home. Another poster that was put up on the wall showed a picture of the Bisto Twins advertising Bisto, a ready-made gravy that, of course, is still available today.

The poster on the wall opposite our home. (Pictorial Press Ltd/ Alamy)

★★★

In April 1940 the government announced that air-raid shelters were to be built at a distance of a hundred or so yards along every street in cities and towns most likely to be bombed. In preparation, large piles of bricks, 20–30ft long and about 6ft high, were deposited along the streets. By then Richard and I were old enough to play in the streets behind the shop, and we knew all the kids who lived within half a mile of our home. John and Renee Curtis were about my age and lived in a big old house that was dark and bereft of much furniture, as their family were poor. Mrs Curtis was a worn-out lady who I never saw in any clothes other than a faded old dress covered by a faded apron. Mr Curtis, by contrast, was a proud railway man, possibly the driver of an important train if the smart black uniform he wore, complete with cap and shining black boots and knee-high leather gaiters, was anything to go by. I never saw him but with a pipe in his mouth, drawing contentedly upon it, as he walked home silently along the street after a day's work.

Behind their house, the Curtises had a long garden at the far end of which was a large wooden shed in which there were a few gardening tools and a large rocking horse. How I envied John and Renee that rocking horse! My parents never bought me anything like that. It was painted off-white, dappled with smudged black spots, and it had a blond mane and running boards on either side from which to mount it, which I did whenever the opportunity presented.

The piles of bricks in the street were ideal for play-ing on, and during the long, light summer evenings that occurred at that time as a result of double British summer time, we had a great time making houses and forts in the bricks, from which we lobbed bits of brick towards the kids on the next pile along the street, although there was no danger of hitting them as we were too far apart.

Other kids joined Richard and me and the Curtises on our pile of bricks. Betty and Margaret were sisters who lived over the shop next door to our shop. Lawrence Osborne was a kid from an adjoining street.

'Let's get that piece of plywood I saw in the garden of number 47 and use it to make a roof. Then we can put bricks over it and make it strong!' one of us shouted one day.

We grabbed the piece of wood without being apprehended and placed it over the walls of bricks we had made. Then we sat crouching in the small dark chamber that resulted, as happy as if we had bought a new house.

Dad had converted one of the two garages behind the shop into a workshop, and with his help, Richard and I made wooden swords and shields, although instead we sometimes used dustbin lids as shields with which to protect ourselves in case the enemy on the next pile of bricks should be so ill advised as to try to invade us.

Apart from the bricks, the government had large steel water tanks placed at strategic points for use by the fire service in the event of bombs setting buildings on fire. In the summer, the tanks made excellent swimming pools in which to cool off, although subsequently they were covered by steel netting to prevent children getting into them after several drowned.

***

One day, when I was 6 or 7, I suddenly had an idea about how babies were conceived, although I had no idea of sex. By then, I was big enough to pee into the toilet at home without difficulty and, as I was standing there doing my stuff, the thought occurred to me that babies are conceived by the mixing of a man and a woman's urine. Of course, my idea was incorrect, but for an uninformed kid it wasn't so wide of the mark, and perhaps suggests that we have innate knowledge about sex.

★★★

We were now old enough to understand what our parents expected of us. We were loved and indulged by both Mum and Dad, and were free to play in and roam the streets close to where we lived, but both our parents had very clear ideas about the way we were to be brought up. Dad was my role model and, in retrospect, the main source of my conscience. He was also the person who imbued both Richard and me with very clear ideas of right and wrong to which we still adhere.

'You are not simply to follow what other boys do,' he insisted on many occasions. 'You are to think for yourselves and do what you know to be right.'

Although we had a lot of freedom, certain things were forbidden, and we risked three across the hand or backside if we did them. So that there should be no misunderstanding, a list of transgressions was placed on a wall by the gas stove in the kitchen, with a cane beside it that we meddled with at our peril. Although we weren't often caned, there was a short period Richard was caned by Mum almost every day. Usually, we probably deserved some form of punishment when we were caned. Mum used to say that we were good immediately after a caning, but gradually worked up to another one after about six to eight weeks, which was probably a bit more frequent than happened in reality.

When Dad caned us, he expected us to be friends immediately afterwards. 'You've received your punishment. Now don't do it again, and let us be friends,' he would say. Sometimes we cried after a caning, but at other times we showed our contempt by grimacing and walking away. The family had a dog, a blue roan cocker spaniel named Bingo, who had been given to me as a birthday present. He was my pal and understood when I had had a caning. He would nuzzle up close to me and, with his chops resting on my thigh, would look up at me with his large black eyes, as if to say, 'I know you are hurting.'

Items on the list of things that could earn us a caning included being caught riding a bike, as a boy who had lived in the flat over a shop named Boatfields, across the road from us, had been killed by a car while riding a bike. Other things on the list included smoking, lying, fighting each other, failing to do as we were told and playing ball in the garden at the back of the shop and breaking the flowers Mum had so lovingly grown.

At this time in our lives, Richard and I fought a lot. We competed over almost everything, from who had the biggest portion at mealtimes to whose turn it was to wash up and whose to wipe up. If we could argue, we did argue. It was as if we were Cain and Abel. Often our arguments ended in fights. Our arguing and fighting upset Mum and Dad a lot, and if we argued for too long in their presence, we would very firmly be told to desist; if we persisted, we would be given a caning.

Because Mum was so busy with the shop, we were expected to do certain jobs. I had to prepare Bingo's meals of biscuit and tinned meat every morning, and take him for a walk in the morning before school and in the evening before we went to bed. Sometimes the butcher would give us a few scraps for him. On one occasion he got out from the shop, where he used to sit with Mum, and trotted up to the butchers. He managed to steal a leg of lamb and come running home with it dangling from his mouth, the butcher shouting behind him.

Although Bingo was my pal, he knew how to play me up. If I let him off the lead when we were walking along a street, he would disappear into a garden and ignore my calls to come out. If it happened on night walks he would evade me for a long time, as often I didn't know which garden he had run into. But he knew who was boss when Dad took him for a walk. It was as if he was glued to Dad's heel. He didn't deviate for so much as a moment. He knew who he had to obey, and who he could fool about with.

If we were at home, Richard and I were required to lay the table and wash up, and had to peel the potatoes when we were somewhat older. We were also expected to sweep the garden at the back of the shop, and the pavement at the front, which I hated doing, as I was self-conscious and embarrassed by the thought that passers-by might look down upon me for doing what I considered to be menial work. Of all the tasks we were expected to do, the one I hated most was 'oiling the blacks', as it involved using oil to polish and buff up the black panels beneath the shop windows while people walked past me.

We were also expected to help by running errands to the shops in the parade where we lived. When we came home from school, we would go into the shop to see Mum, and hopefully be allowed to go upstairs and have a couple of slices of bread and jam or bread and dripping. In return, if she wanted any shopping, she would send us to one of the local shops with a list that might contain up to seven or eight items.

All this may sound as if our childhood was overburdened with jobs and things we were forbidden to do, but it wasn't so, as we knew that Mum was busy in the shop and needed help. Also, we liked going to the various shops she sent us to, and appreciated that the rules we were expected to follow were clear and gave us boundaries within which we were free.

★★★

Mum had her favourite shops, but to keep on good terms with all the local shopkeepers, she would occasionally send us to less-favoured ones. The shop immediately next door was a grocers that belonged to a chain named Bishops. It was efficiently run by Betty and Margaret's dad, and was bright and clean, but for some reason it wasn't one of Mum's favourites, which was just as well as shopping there could take a long time as goods were sold from two counters and, depending upon what you wanted, you might have to queue at both. On one side of the shop, Mr Bradford sold consumables such as cheese, butter and bacon. On the other, Mrs Bradford and a lady named Gwen sold non-perishables such as tinned foods, sugar, jams and breakfast cereals.

Next to Bradford's was a newsagents run by a miserable, bald, grey-faced man named Mr Goswell. He was belligerent and expressed views almost as extreme as those in the newspapers he sold.

Mum's favourite shop for groceries was Elborns, but occasionally we were sent to Bennett's, a grocers on the other side of the main road on which we lived. It was similar with the butcher's shop. Her favourite butcher was Pearce's, but every now and again we were sent to Young's, run by a husband and wife.

Elborns was run by a married couple, who, unsurprisingly, were named Mr and Mrs Elborn. Both were old and bent, and their shop was old-fashioned and a mess. They moved slowly from counter to counter amid unpacked boxes of such things as breakfast cereals and HP sauce. Mr Elborn wore a white jacket and a white apron that was stained and only occasionally changed. The best that could be said of their shop was that it was Victorian.

Bennett's, by contrast, was bright and spruce. Mr Bennett was well over 6ft tall and had thick red lips and thick black, Brylcreemed hair, combed straight back. He was business-like, and was often to be seen counting out rashers of bacon from a pile resting in the palm of his enormous hand. But as I have said, for some odd reason, Mum preferred muddly old Elborns.

Pearce was an excellent butchers run by two smiling, early middle-aged men with loud voices. They joked with customers, and were very different to Mr Young of Young's, the other butchers. Mr Young was old and had a pink unblemished face topped by a mop of very white hair. Mrs Young looked like a lady from a Victorian photograph, with her hair gathered up in a bun on top of her head. Usually she sat in a cashier's box in the middle of their shop. Mum preferred Pearce's, and I was always uncomfortable when I was sent to Young's as they were snooty and offhand with me because, I suspected, they didn't like the fact that Mum didn't buy all our family's meat from them.

There was even a first-class fishmongers displaying fresh fillets of cod, haddock and plaice in the parade of shops on the other side of the main road. Sharvells smelled unpleasantly of the chemicals given off by fish. The Sharvells had a 7-year-old son named Peter, who had a short left leg due to a congenitally dislocated hip that caused him to hobble, despite several operations, and he wore a boot with a sole about 6in thick. I felt guilty and sorry each time I saw Peter, and tried to be especially friendly towards him because I could walk normally but he couldn't, and he couldn't come out to play with us.

Other shops in the parade included Olivers, the baker; Goodalls, the chemist; and a dairy belonging to a chain of dairies named the Express Dairies that delivered milk to the home by horse-drawn cart.

★★★

At mealtimes, Richard and I were expected to eat everything that was put down in front of us. I loved fried sausages, onions fried in sugar, baked beans, mashed potatoes and chips, and would gladly have filled up on them at any time. By contrast, I hated fish, boiled or fried eggs with watery yolks, broccoli and Brussels sprouts. When Mum served them, I was not allowed to leave the table until I had eaten them. If I persisted in being unable to do so, sometimes they were brought out for my next meal. On one occasion, Richard and I were kept sitting at the meal table for more than an hour, staring and retching over a plate of haddock cooked in milk and butter that we just could not eat. Lunch on Friday was particularly difficult, as the nation was still fairly religious and people omitted meat and ate fish on that day in order to identify with Jesus' sacrifice on the cross. Our family did not follow any particular faith, but perhaps because Dad had been brought up as a Catholic, we followed the convention and, much to the chagrin of Richard and me, we usually ate fish on Friday.

The only type of fish I liked was fish and chips from the fish and chip shop in the parade of shops on the other side of the road. It was off ration, and if Mum didn't want to cook, she would send me, or Richard when he was a little older, across the road to get dinner for the family. It was delicious! Cooked in batter, an ordinary-sized piece of cod or haddock cost 6d, or 2½p in today's money. A larger piece cost 9d, and a bag of chips 3d. Plaice was a little more expensive. Best was to salt and vinegar whatever we'd ordered and eat it from the newspaper in which it had been wrapped.

If Mum and Dad weren't looking while we were eating, I would slip Bingo bits of meat and the foods I didn't like, such as fish and vegetables, and he would lick them up from the floor, although even he wouldn't eat Brussels sprouts or broccoli. If either Mum or Dad saw me feeding him during a meal, they would say something along the lines of, 'If you do that again, it will be Bingo who gets a slap, not you!' which of course made me wary and watchful about continuing to feed him for the remaining part of that meal.

Feeding Bingo at table was not the only situation in which he could be punished on my behalf. At night I liked to push him down inside the bedcovers to the bottom of my bed so that I could put my feet on him and use him like a hot water bottle. He didn't mind, but Mum did. 'He's making the sheets black. If you do that again, it will be Bingo who gets a slap, not you,' she said. So after that I was careful, and after warming my feet on him, would bring him up and let him jump onto the floor to be sure of escaping Mum's wrath.

# 4

# THE SHOOTING
# WAR BEGINS

On 10 May 1940 our lives suddenly changed. As I sat listening to the radio in the kitchen of our flat above the shop, I learnt that Germany had attacked France and the Low Countries. The Phoney War was over, and the shooting and killing war had begun.

Following the First World War, the French had built a line of forts known as the Maginot Line to protect their border from Germany. Surprisingly, so far as I can ascertain, they did not extend it behind the border they shared with Belgium. The British had invented the tank during the First World War, but it was the Germans who exploited it to such effect during that summer of 1940, and later, in 1941 against Russia. Attacking where it was least expected by the Allies, German tanks poured through the Ardennes in the south of Belgium and, skirting round the north of the Maginot Line, entered France in what was known as *Blitzkrieg*, meaning 'lightning war'.

A British Expeditionary Force had been sent to the aid of the French, but the *Blitzkrieg* was a new form of war that was difficult to withstand. Within a short time, the Allied armies were outmanoeuvred and forced to retreat. The situation worsened, and on 26 May a plan known as Operation Dynamo was put into action by the British, with the aim of fighting a rearguard action and rescuing as many of the surrounded British and French forces as possible and bringing them back to Britain. After this, on 22 June, France capitulated and the Germans swaggered into Paris.

I was old enough to know that the situation was dire, and that it was likely that Britain might be invaded. I felt threatened and was frightened. The *Nine O'Clock News* on the BBC Home Service was our main source of information. Each evening, along with almost the entire nation, Richard, Mum, Dad and I gathered around the family's radio in the kitchen and listened anxiously to the day's news and the list of the latest disasters.

The main piece of news was that our troops had retreated towards the port of Dunkirk, where they were trapped with their backs to the sea. If the Germans managed to advance any further our men would be pushed into the water and would be annihilated, drowned or captured. All that remained between them and disaster was a rapidly assembled fleet of Allied destroyers, merchant ships, fishing boats and small boats manned by their civilian owners – the Little Ships of Dunkirk – that sailed across the English Channel from the south-east corner of England in a bid to rescue the army.

Many of the vessels that went to Dunkirk were yachts and motorboats of the type used for recreation at weekends. Mr Ferris owned a small cabin cruiser and was among them, although the engine of his boat broke down before he reached the open sea. As they approached the French coast, the armada was machine-gunned and bombed from the air. On the beaches they were met by long lines of exhausted troops, many standing almost up to their necks in the sea, waiting to see if they would be rescued or left behind to the mercy of the Germans. By the standards of any normal logic it was a hopeless situation, but the sea was calm, and somehow, by good fortune and courage, the small boats and the larger Allied ships rescued an incredible 350,000 men and brought them back to the safety of England, and in doing so turned certain defeat into a glorious victory of a very special British kind – although, as Mr Churchill said, 'Wars are not won by evacuations.'

For Richard and me it was both a frightening and an exciting time. As boys, we played at being soldiers, and that was exciting; but at the same time, in the way that a calf will respond to its mother's moods, I felt Mum and Dad's apprehension. Only 20 miles away across the sea, the bully boys were marshalling their forces and preparing to invade. Mum was Jewish, and goodness knows what would have happened to us if they had succeeded.

The Germans, of course, were cock-a-hoop. Sometimes after meals, we sat around the radio and listened to 'Lord Haw-Haw' (William Joyce), a British traitor who had opted for the German side, broadcast in English from Germany. His broadcasts started with the words, 'Germany calling, Germany calling …' His programmes were propaganda of the crudest type and were interspaced with music. As I listened, I heard German soldiers singing martial songs as

they strutted all over Europe. The songs were loud and triumphant. Apparently, it had not occurred to them or their
masters that they had no right to other people's lands. They
simply looked upon the Poles and Slavs they had conquered
as *Untermensch* – subhuman – and the Jews as even less. One
of Lord Haw-Haw's favourite songs went:

> Good bye England, your golden days are over.
> Good bye England, your golden days are over …

By way of riposte, Richard and I and our friends sang a
little ditty that was known to many British children at
that time:

> Where was the engine driver when the boiler burst?
> He was singing:
> Hitler has only got one ball
> Göring has two, but one's too small
> Himmler has something similar
> But poor old Goebbels has no balls at all

Another little ditty we sang, while imitating the goose
step, was:

> When the Führer says we are the Master Race, we hail
> phumph! hail phumph! Right in his bloody face!

★★★

In July the Germans started to bomb RAF airfields in
the southern half of England. Then, on 7 September,
having failed to eliminate the RAF, the Germans began

the systematic bombing of London and other cities throughout the UK in what became known as the Blitz. Almost every night for eight months, swarms of German bombers zoomed about like angry wasps over London and other cities, dropping high explosives and incendiary bombs. Their main targets in London were the docks in the East End, but they also bombed other targets throughout the city. There was a large railway marshalling yard and a power station about 500 yards from our home, and on many occasions the Germans attempted to hit them without success, their bombs destroying homes and killing and maiming people close by. On a couple of occasions, high-explosive bombs fell within 200–300 yards of our home, and on one occasion, as close as 100 yards, blowing out the flat windows, petrifying Bingo and terrifying us humans.

Each night we slept in our air-raid shelter, where we were joined by Rita and Mrs Ferris. Usually Mr Ferris and Dad were on duty. Mr Ferris owned a dairy, but volunteered to be a fireman at the outbreak of war. On many occasions he was sent to the City of London, the East End or the Docks, and often was surrounded by fires on all sides, and was in danger of burning buildings collapsing on him, as he fought fires raging in many parts of London. On one occasion, he was buried beneath rubble, but fortunately was dug out and rescued. Dad also had several narrow escapes. One morning he was sent to North Wembley to guard the site where a landmine – a large bomb delivered by parachute – had fallen. At two o'clock a colleague relieved him. Half an hour later, the bomb exploded killing the colleague, who was a personal friend of Dad.

St Paul's Cathedral surrounded by fire and smoke. (World Image Archive/Alamy)

When Dad was off duty and at home for a night with the family in the shelter, he would go to the entrance if the bombing was severe but not too close and would call Richard and me to come up and join him so we could see what was happening. On several occasions I saw a red glow and flames leaping up into the sky to the east, where the City of London and the docks were on fire. On other occasions I saw the white beams of searchlights criss-crossing the sky as they searched for enemy planes.

The sound of German planes overhead became so common that when an aeroplane approached, I could tell if it was a Jerry or one of ours from the sound emitted by its engines. German planes were tuned in such a way that they made a droning sound that waxed and waned. 'That's a Jerry!' or 'Jerry's here again!' I would say, as I stood looking up into the sky from the entrance to the shelter, as every few seconds, the engines of an approaching plane became alternately louder and softer. Hopefully, the droning would fade, indicating that the plane was moving away, in which case, if she heard it, Mum would say something such as, 'Some other poor devils are going to cop it tonight.'

One night in late 1940, the siren sounded at about half past seven. Bingo was the first of our family to acknowledge it. He had learnt that the sound emitted by the air-raid siren indicated that an air raid was about to occur, and when he heard it, he rushed to the front door of the flat and sat whimpering and scratching the door until one of us opened it for him. At this point he rushed headlong down to the shelter, followed by Richard and me in our pyjamas and dressing gowns, and Mum in her everyday clothes with a shopping bag containing a thermos flask of tea and some sandwiches and biscuits, in case the raid lasted for several hours. Our route to the shelter took us down the stairs from the flat, across our back garden and the forecourt of the two garages that Mum and Dad owned, and finally onto the square of land on which the shelter had been built. Once there, we hurtled down the shelter's steps and into the damp-smelling safety of its interior. Only then did we feel reasonably safe.

The shelter was like a small underground room. It was fitted with electric light, and its thick concrete walls and steel and concrete roof felt like a tortoise's shell around me. Once in it, we huddled in a row on the lower of the two wooden bunks Dad had made, and sat waiting to learn what would happen.

We did not have long to wait. Within a minute or two the echoing boom of anti-aircraft guns started up, becoming louder and louder, indicating that at least one enemy plane was approaching, and was getting closer and closer.

A few seconds later I heard the waxing and waning sound of a German aircraft. Jerry was very near. A moment later I heard footsteps on the steps leading down into the shelter, and a few seconds later we were joined by Mrs Ferris in her everyday clothes and Rita in her pyjamas and dressing gown. Both had rushed across the road when they heard the booming of the guns.

'It looks as if it's going to be a dreadful night. Jerry's very early today, don't you think?' Mum said, shifting along the bunk to make room for Mrs Ferris.

The droning of the aeroplane and the booming of the guns became so loud that it sounded as if the shells they were firing were exploding right over our heads. I braced myself. I was very frightened. In my chest, I could feel my heart banging and a pulse beating at the back of my throat. Alongside me, I was vaguely aware of Mum praying aloud, and saying. 'Please, dear God, if you spare us tonight, I will go to church every Sunday,' which was hardly appropriate, as she was Jewish!

I huddled up in my dressing gown and curled up in fear, waiting for the explosions I expected to occur at any moment. Was I about to die and be blown to bits? I could not think of anything other than that I might be killed.

At the next moment there was a distant plop, followed by another, louder and nearer, and then another, louder and nearer still. Jerry had dropped a stick of bombs, and they were coming straight at us. An explosion occurred after each plop and, as they grew louder and louder, they sounded like plop, explosion … plop, explosion … plop, explosion … plop, explosion …

With the last explosion the ground shook, the shelter shuddered, and the hurricane lamp that hung from the wall swung back and forth on its hook. I was no longer able to think. I was just a bag of terrified fear.

Then it was over, and there was just the booming of the guns ...

We had survived. We were alive. Jerry had passed on and had gone elsewhere, at least for the moment.

We took stock. We were all very weak and shaken.

'That was a close one,' one of us children said.

'Thank God we've been spared!' Mrs Ferris exclaimed. 'I don't think I can take much more of this.'

Mum gave each of us a biscuit and a cup of tea, and eventually we settled down for the night. We three children were covered with blankets on the lower bunk, Mrs Ferris was on the top bunk, and Mum was on a camp bed that she had erected on the remaining floor space.

Because they were smaller than me, Richard and Rita were put at one end of the lower bunk and I was at the other.

Richard tickled Rita, and I pushed her feet away.

'Stop it!' she said, striking out with her fists. 'I hate you. You're both beastly boys!'

'Your feet smell, that's why I pushed them away!' I snapped.

Rita began to cry, but I didn't care. I simply turned over and went to sleep. Being nasty to her helped relieve some of the tension within me.

★★★

Next morning on our way to school, like hundreds of children all over London, Richard and I scoured the pavements and gutters for pieces of bomb and shell. It was a competitive business, both between Richard and me and the other children who lived nearby. Within the three or four minutes that it took us to get to school, we each had four or five pieces of jagged metal that we placed in brown paper bags we had brought with us specially for the purpose. Some of the bits were made of brass, others of steel. Once I found a piece that was about 4in long and would have killed anyone it dropped on.

In the calm of the morning, they were surreal reminders of the horror and destruction of the previous night.

★★★

Two or three nights later, Dad, who was off duty for the night, called Richard and me up from the shelter at about ten o'clock to see an enemy plane.

'See that searchlight beam over there?' he asked, pointing to a thin pencil of white light shining up into the sky. 'Follow it up towards the small cloud you can see, and tell me what you see.'

We did as he bid us. Where the light scraped the bottom of the cloud, I could see the bright white outline of an aircraft high up in the sky, just below the cloud.

'That's a German,' Dad said. 'Once they've caught them like that, they never escape.'

I watched the flak bursting about the plane, and thought of the men inside it. Something in me told me that they were men like I might be one day, and I felt sorry for them as they panicked and tried to escape, and fought with the realisation that they were likely to be killed.

★★★

Over the following nights the bombing became so bad that Mum and Dad decided they had to do something about it.

Dad found and rented a room in a large house on the main square of Buckingham, the county town of Buckinghamshire, a train journey of about 50 miles in a north-westerly direction from London. The owner of the house was a kindly elderly lady named Mrs Noabes. About three times a week, after the shop closed, Mum gathered up us boys and the dog, and with a bag of food, we set out on a short walk to the bus stop; then by No. 83 bus to Wembley Park Station; and after that, by train to Buckingham. Goodness knows how Mum could face such a journey, or had the energy to make it after a day's work, as the streets, the bus, the railway station and the carriages of the train were all barely lit due to the blackout. It was like making a journey through the negative of a film. At every step there was the danger of tripping or falling over, but Mum thought it was worthwhile in order that we might be safe for the night and get a good night's sleep.

The house where we stayed was named Old Hall, and is still in the High Street today. Mrs Noabes was well over 80, and was so bent that, when she stood up or walked, her head and neck were almost parallel with the ground. Like many old ladies at that time, she wore a long, heavy, black skirt that reached down to her feet, a black top, and had her hair, which was white, done up in a bun at the back of her head. She was kind and wanted to help, and each week gave her sweet ration to Richard and me.

As far as I remember, the hall of the house was dominated by a grand dark wooden staircase that snaked up round its walls to the top floor. The rooms where we slept were large, high-ceilinged, barn-like spaces that belonged to a past era. Before we went to bed, Mrs Noabes inserted a round copper bed warmer, filled with hot water and mounted on a long wooden pole, into each of our beds. In each bedroom there was a large jug of water standing in a china bowl in which we washed our face and hands in the morning. Usually, the water in the jugs was cold, but sometimes Mrs Noabes brought up a succession of kettles filled with hot water for us.

Outside the house, the town square was cobbled, and when we got up on Thursday mornings there was a cattle market outside the dining room window, replete with fenced animal pens in which there were cows snorting steam from their nostrils on cold mornings.

After a breakfast of cereal, toast and marmalade, and coffee, Mum rounded us up and herded us back to London on the reverse journey by train and bus, arriving just in time for school, and for Mum to start another day's work in the shop.

# 5

# LIFE AT WAR

One of the most striking features about life during the war was how normal it was for much of the time for most of the population. In a way it was similar to a soldier's life, with periods of intense action, fear and excitement interspersed with periods of inaction. After a night of bombing, most people who weren't directly involved went to work and about their ordinary daytime lives in much the same way as they had before the war. Children went to school, people fell in love, others went on holidays, and still others died of natural causes. Of course, there were worries about relatives who were away in the armed forces, particularly if they were abroad and involved in fighting, but otherwise life went on in its usual way. People gossiped. The war was their main topic of discussion, but they also talked about their children, their gardens, their pets and the hundred and one things that people talk about. Mr Goswell, the bald, pessimistic owner of the newsagent store next door but one to Mum's shop, said to anyone who would listen, 'I don't like it one little bit. I think Hitler will be here by Christmas, and then what will happen to us? All I can say is, "God help us all."' Apart from when he was serving in the shop, he spent most of his time sitting with his wife in arm-chairs in the well-appointed lounge at the back, although occasionally he would emerge to go for an early morning or late evening walk, wearing a cap to cover his bald-ness. One night in the darkness caused by the blackout, as Dad was walking home from night duty, he fell over one of the wooden trestles that Mr Goswell had placed on the pavement to advertise the newspapers he sold. Dad broke his arm and was in plaster and off duty for almost two months. By way of apology, Mr Goswell promised to remove the trestles, but they were back on the pavement outside his shop within a matter of weeks.

Probably because the country's situation was so bleak, the people pulled together in a way they had not done before the war. The radio and the newspapers helped this. Apart from listening to the news on the BBC, prac-tically the whole nation listened to Winston Churchill's speeches, and to *It's That Man Again,* a radio comedy that was broadcast every Thursday evening at half past eight. If you listen to *ITMA* now it sounds silly and not very funny, but during the war the nation rocked with laughter as it listened to Tommy Handley and Jack Train, and a host of imaginary characters such as Fumf, the German spy; Colonel Chinstrap, who came on each week saying 'I say, Sir. I don't mind if I do ...'; and Mrs Mopp, the cleaner, whose call line was, 'Can I do you now, Sir?' The next day people asked each other if they had heard the programme and its jokes, and laughed again as they repeated them to one another. The singer Vera Lynn also kept up the nation's spirits, singing to the people at home and troops abroad. Her voice had a unique quality of longing about it, and her songs such as 'The White Cliffs of Dover' and 'I'll Be Seeing You' are still played today.

When the bombs weren't falling, like most children of the time, Richard and I got as much satisfaction from the games we improvised for ourselves as we did from the few toys that Mum and Dad could afford and were available. Cars was one of our favourite games; it was played largely in our imaginations, and did not cost a thing. What we did was place a kitchen chair with its back on the floor of the kitchen. We would then pretend that its back was the seat of a car; that the seat of the chair, which was sticking up at right angles to the floor, was the dashboard and driving wheel; and that the legs extending out in front of it were the bonnet. Sitting on the back of the chair, for hours we pretended that we were racing car drivers, weaving in and out of imaginary traffic. Eighty years later, I still get great pleasure from similar simple pastimes, such as walking in the countryside or cycling around London on my electric bike.

On wet afternoons, another of our favourite pastimes was looking at the books Dad had collected. Most of Mum and Dad's reading matter came from the public library, but over the years, Dad had collected a couple of hundred books that he kept in a bookcase he had made. As we were only rarely allowed in the front room where they were kept, Mum brought them out to us in the kitchen, where we spent hours looking at them. Among the books I liked most was a series of orange-coloured, bound magazines called *Our Wonderful World* that Dad had collected on a monthly basis prior to having them bound. In them were splendid pictures of great liners such as the *Queen Mary* and the *Normandie*, and a picture taken in a museum of a mammoth sitting on its haunches, as its bottom had been eaten away by the dogs that had drawn the sledges of the party that had discovered it in the ice in northern Siberia. Apparently, its flesh had been so fresh that it had been almost impossible to stop the hungry animals savaging its backside. Another picture I liked was one of a man standing perilously balanced against the skyline as, several hundred feet above the ground, he worked from the top of a ladder that was leaning against a telegraph pole protruding from the roof of a skyscraper in New York. You could tell that it was taken in the 1930s by the voluminous shape of his cap and the bagginess of his trousers. Another of my favourites, was the picture of a tiny statue of a sophisticated woman living in Ur of the Chaldeans in the ninth century BCE. Although it was almost 3,000 years old, quite incredibly, it looked as if it was the recently crafted representation of a sophisticated modern woman. She was beautifully dressed. The front of her chest was bare and her waist was so small that it looked as if she was wearing a corset.

Among the books in the bookcase were a complete set of Gibbon's *Decline and Fall of the Roman Empire*, Bernard Shaw's *Man and Superman*, Tolstoy's *War and Peace* and Spinoza's *Ethics*, as well as a slim soft-covered volume titled *The Red Light*, in which was all the information about sex that it was then thought the general public needed to know. At the time, it was a rather notorious little publication that was hidden away in most homes, particularly if there were children in the house. It contained diagrams and descriptions of human genitalia and instructions on how to make love. Naturally, Richard and I read it, or rather looked at it with great interest, and speculated that our parents would not be so foolish as to do any of the things recommended in its pages. Another book that Dad had collected was Hitler's *Mein Kampf* – meaning 'my struggle' – but as it was in German and old Gothic print, I was unable to read it. In retrospect, I can only guess that Dad bought it when he, Mum and I were on the hiking holiday during which he carried me in a carry chair along the River Rhine in Germany in 1934.

★★★

Apart from playing in the kitchen, when the weather was good enough, and if we weren't at school, Richard and I often played in the streets. Because of the war, there weren't many cars on the roads and, as there was little awareness at that time of child abduction or the sexual abuse of children, the streets were considered safe to play in. Cricket and football were our favourite games, with stumps or goalposts drawn in chalk on the wall of a house in Swinderby Road, a side road less than 100 yards from our home. Another favourite was playing with Betty and Margaret, the girls from next door, on the swings and roundabouts in a local park named One Tree Hill. Adjoining it was a piece of wasteland that we children called the Old Field. Today the Old Field is a flat piece of uninteresting mowed grassland, but until well after the war it was covered with trees that we climbed and bushes in which we hid, built camps and played cowboys and Indians or cops and robbers. On dozens of occasions, I sat in the middle of a clump of bushes in the Old Field, hoping that I would not be found.

Betty and Margaret were about the same age as us, and if we weren't playing in the streets or in the park we were likely to be playing houses or mothers and fathers in their back yard, or if the weather was wet, Monopoly in their kitchen. Like many homes at that time, the girls' home stank of body odour that in retrospect I think was due to a combination of the national habit of bathing only once a week (showers were almost unknown in Britain at that time), and in many homes only occasionally opening windows, so that the air became stale and smelly. I had other friends whose homes had the same odour, and the secondary school I eventually went to stank of adolescent boys for the same reasons. Apart from not opening windows, another reason that homes and places like schools stank was that in general people washed their hair only once every three or so weeks in the belief that washing it more frequently would wash out the natural oils; hence, combined with bathing only once a week, the term 'the great unwashed'!

I loved playing Monopoly. Each of us children had our favourite properties. I liked hotels on Park Lane and Mayfair. Richard and the girls liked Piccadilly and Leicester Square and the properties that were coloured green, such as Regent Street. Sometimes I won and sometimes I lost, and in the process learnt tolerance and that in this life you can't have everything you want.

On Monday mornings the girls' kitchen was transformed into the family's laundry. Against one of its walls was a laundry tub, a large galvanised metal drum like a dustbin on four legs. At the appointed hour, one of the girls filled the tub with water, then their mother, Mrs Bradford, a buxom woman in her forties who laughed a lot and was full of the joys of life, lit a small coal fire under it, and along with a quantity of soap flakes, boiled the family's laundry for a couple of hours or so. Afterwards, each piece of laundry was fed through the rollers of a mangle – an upright cast iron contraption on which there were two large, rubberised rollers from which each piece emerged almost dry and as flat as a piece of rolled out pastry, ready to be hung out on the washing line in the yard at the back of the shop. Our Mum was too busy to wash our laundry at home. Instead, she bundled it up and got one of us boys to take it across the road to the Advance Laundry, where it was washed and ironed, and returned to us during the following week.

★★★

At home, Richard and I had to watch our table manners and the way we spoke.

'Don't drop your aitches ... If you don't speak more carefully, you'll have to have elocution lessons, and you won't be able to go out to play with the local children anymore.'

If I heard Dad say that once, I heard him say it a dozen times. But although he was able to take us to task over our speech, he wasn't able to teach us proper table manners, as his mother had died when he was young and he hadn't had anyone to teach him about such things. So, it was Mum who taught us table manners.

'Close your mouth when you eat, and don't speak with your mouth full!' she said repeatedly, as we sat eating at the kitchen table. 'Don't put your elbows on the table!' and 'How many more times have I got to tell you to use your fork properly and not like a shovel!' Such were the messages that were drilled into us. As a consequence, even today I feel guilty if I turn my fork over the 'wrong way' when eating peas and suchlike.

★★★

But to return to the war. Because Dad used the car to carry goods for Mum's business, he still had a small monthly ration of petrol, although not for long, as shortly afterwards the ration was withdrawn and the car was raised up on wooden chocks for the rest of the war in an attempt to preserve its tyres.

While he still had some petrol, one afternoon during the summer of 1941 Richard and I went with him to collect some dresses from a manufacturer in Ruislip. As we motored along the High Street, we saw several people standing looking up into the sky. So, Dad stopped the car and opened its sunroof to see what was happening. For us on the ground it was an apparently, peaceful summer's afternoon in suburbia, but as we looked up through the roof of the car, very high up against the blue of the sky, we saw Messerschmitts and Spitfires zooming about in a life-and-death struggle, trying to dodge one another, and firing as they tried to shoot each other down – such was the madness of war. Fortunately, nothing untoward happened during the time we were watching, but even so, although I was only 8 years old, I realised that men might be killed in front of my eyes.

★★★

By the middle of 1941 the bombing had become part of our lives. If the siren sounded at six or seven in the evening, people would say, 'Jerry's early tonight,' and if it sounded later, 'Jerry's late tonight.' Because they were so deep, the Underground railway stations in the centre of London became places of refuge, some of which were eventually lined with wooden bunks on which people slept at the back of the platform. Those lucky enough to get a place on a bunk had a reasonably comfortable night; those who didn't had no alternative but to spread their blankets on the hard concrete platform and sleep as best they could. On one evening, when Richard and I were with Mum at Holborn Underground Station at about six o'clock, people on the platform cheered when a man appeared and shouted the good news that a large number of German bombers had been shot down that day. On another occasion, during a quiet period, we went by Underground train with Mum and Dad to Oxford Circus on our way to see the pantomime *Peter Pan*. As we came out of the station, we were greeted by the sound of bombs falling close by. In response, Dad said, 'Quick, boys! Go back down! We're not going out there! Follow me down to the platform as quick as you can!'

Sleeping in London's Underground wasn't entirely without hazard. I remember hearing later in the war about a tragedy that occurred following the sounding of the air-raid siren on a dark night. At Bethnal Green Underground station in the East End, a woman and a child fell near the bottom of the stairs leading into the blacked-out entrance to the station. Within seconds, hundreds of the people following them fell on top of them, and in the resulting crush 173 people were killed. One rumour that I heard myself

People sleeping in the Underground. (Colin Waters/Alamy)

had it that they were mainly Jews and refugees. Maybe it was spread to (wrongly) suggest that the lives of such people were of less value than those of ordinary British citizens, and that because of that, it was less of a tragedy.

★★★

If the bombing was bad, we reverted to the journey by train to Mrs Noabes in Buckingham, but when there was a quiet period, we stayed at home. If the siren sounded when we were at home, our hearts began to pound and, led by Bingo, we rushed down to the shelter with Mum muttering something such as, 'Please, dear God, I promise to be good and pray every day if you spare us and stop the bombs coming closer.' Occasionally, as we sat in the shelter, we would suddenly be left in the dark without any electricity and would fumble around for a torch with which to find a match to light the hurricane lamp, and possibly one of the candles kept in the shelter. Then, if there were explosions close by and the shelter began to shake, our minds would close in upon themselves and our bodies become rigid with fear, as with hearts pounding, we watched the lantern swing back and forth, and the beam of light it cast, swing up and down across the walls of the shelter in response to the vibrations in the earth caused by the explosions.

When Dad was at home and the bombing wasn't too close, he would call Richard and me up out of the shelter so that we could see what was happening. On several occasions, I saw a red glow and a hint of flames leaping up into the sky away to the east, where the City of London and the docks were again burning, but I didn't see any more German aeroplanes caught in searchlight beams.

# 6

# A WAR OF
# CONTRASTS

In the early summer of 1941 the Germans invaded
Russia, and within a few weeks had advanced over
300 miles. The invasion of Russia took the Germans'
attention and resources away from bombing Britain, and
one afternoon during the resulting quiet period, Dad
took Richard and me to the cinema, where during the
Pathé News I saw film of German soldiers cock-a-hoop
and laughing, as they sat enjoying the sun and smoking
in the backs of open lorries carrying them deeper and
deeper into Soviet Russia.

In Wembley, Mum advertised for help in the shop. She
expected a reply from someone young, such as a school
leaver looking for a job. Instead, the person who replied
to the advert and turned up to be interviewed was a tall,
aristocratic-looking, middle-aged lady, who might best be
described as a grande dame. After speaking to her, Mum
explained that the job would probably be too menial for

her, as it involved serving behind a counter in a shop and doing jobs such as dusting and tidying up. But Mrs Gray, as the lady was named, was adamant.

'Please give me a trial,' she pleaded. 'You see, I am worried out of my wits. I have two sons fighting in the war, one in Africa, and the other in the Far East, and I don't know what's happening to them. I can't sleep for worry about them, and I need a job to distract me and take my mind off them, at least for a little while.'

So it was that Mrs Gray, the aristocratic-looking lady whose family were landowners and gentlemen farmers in Norfolk, came to work in the shop for Mum. It seemed unlikely that it would last. But Mrs Gray was a person of great empathy, a lovely lady who learnt quickly and within a few weeks proved to be an excellent saleslady, keen to make as many sales as possible. Within a short time she was part of our world, particularly part of mine. I loved Mrs Gray. She had a beautifully modulated English voice and a ready laugh. She was a big woman, and I can see her now, like a ship under full sail, almost floating along the side street that led from her home to the shop, a hat with a veil over her face and a smart black coat topped by a fur collar over her matronly form. Soon there was a special relationship between us. I felt comfortable in her company and regularly trotted beside her on the way back to her home. She had been bombed out and had rented a bungalow in a street approximately half a mile behind the shop. It had a garden of more than half an acre. Today, such a large garden would be a property developer's dream, as they want only to make as much money as possible by packing in as many homes as they can into a given area. So, now there is an additional bungalow crammed in on either side of what was once Mrs Gray's home. But in those far-off days when the world was simpler, if more dangerous, after I had accompanied her back to her home, and she had given me a cup of tea and a piece of cake, I would ask her if I might play with the guns that hung in her drawing room. They were a boy's dream and I was fascinated by them, as I expect most boys would have been. One was a flintlock pistol with a curved handle of a type dating back to the early sixteenth century. The other was a large steel revolver that had belonged to a German officer during the First World War.

'You must be careful with them, and don't go out into the street with them,' Mrs Gray replied. 'I don't want you frightening the neighbours with guns!'

Holding them carefully, I took them into the garden and, full of respect for them, rolled the barrel of the revolver round with my thumb, and pointed it first at an imaginary target and then at several others.

During several summers, I spent many happy hours playing contentedly in that garden. Quite apart from the guns, it was a super place for a boy to play. It contained flower beds; a large clump of pampas grass, some of which was 6 or 7ft tall; a summer house tucked away in a corner; and a pond in which water lilies grew. The summerhouse was furnished with a sofa and an armchair, and was pervaded by an unused, musty smell of decay that, although I was young, filled me with an intangible feeling of regret and sadness for the past. Sitting quietly in the armchair, it wasn't difficult for me to imagine the Edwardian men and women who had sat there on hot summer afternoons long ago. They had been as alive and real as I was. What had happened to them, I wondered?

Where were they now? Where had they gone? The answers to such questions still elude me, although I am open to the possibility that perhaps it is beyond our minds to understand such things.

In the spring and early summer, I lay on my stomach by the pond and inspected clumps of frogspawn that looked like semi-transparent bunches of grapes with little black pips in their centres. Later, I watched the tadpoles that emerged from the pips become little black frogs with tails that gradually shortened and disappeared. Once or twice, I collected some spawn in a jam jar and took it home and, together with Richard and Dad, watched it gradually develop into little frogs that, I have to confess, invariably died.

Each month, Mrs Gray went by train for a weekend with her family in Norfolk and, on returning to the shop on Monday afternoon, came proudly wafting along the road carrying a basket that might contain a duck, a dozen eggs, or perhaps a rabbit or pheasant for us. All these things, of course, were gifts and off ration. With the approach of winter, I helped Mum pickle some of the eggs in a slimy pickling fluid and store them in a bucket so that we had a supply during the winter when Mrs Gray made fewer trips to the country.

I was old enough to understand when, one day, Mum told me that Mrs Gray was unhappily married. 'Mr Gray is a distant man, an unpleasant cold fish who's wrapped up in his work as the editor of a literary magazine and the writer of children's stories,' Mum said. 'And as a consequence, Mrs Gray feels ignored and unloved.'

★★★

As the war continued and Richard and I grew bigger, our different personalities began to appear. It became apparent that I was a serious, quiet child, whereas Richard had a sunny personality and was gregarious. In some ways, the differences between us seem to fit with a psychological theory I read about in a book concerned with the development of children. According to the theory, about which I have an open mind, the pressures and anxieties of being a parent for the first time have a tendency to communicate themselves to their firstborn who, as a result, may be prone to anxiety and a need to prove themselves in a way that makes them driven. By contrast, by the time the second child is born, the parents are typically more relaxed and confident about child-rearing, and as a consequence, often the second child feels less pressurised, and is more likely to be outgoing than the first. At any rate, that's how it seemed to be with Richard and me.

I have a picture in my mind of myself at this time. In it, I see myself as a long, thin, dark-haired child with an appearance that I did not like. I was so thin that Mum and Dad called me 'Tinribs', or sometimes 'Hollow Legs' on account of my voracious appetite for the things I liked, such as mashed potatoes, baked beans and fried sausages. At school, I was good at maths and sciences, although I wasn't good at reading and didn't manage to read more than the first twenty or so pages of Arthur Ransome's books *Swallows and Amazons* and *We Didn't Mean to Go to Sea*. Usually, I came home with good reports, although there were exceptions when I did not please a particular teacher.

In contrast to me, Richard was fair-haired and extroverted. Although we both had lots of friends of our own and shared several others, such as Rita Ferris and Betty and Margaret, at the back of my mind, I think it is possible that I envied Richard his friends. To an extent, his priorities were different to mine and lay outside the classroom, although he was always the first to offer help to a teacher if there was any tidying up to be done after class. Most boys, including me, have no love for soap and water and washing themselves, but Richard had a particular aversion. If Mum or Dad suspected he had done no more than rub himself with a towel when he was supposed to have washed himself, he would be sent back to the bathroom to wash himself properly. Bathing wasn't much of a problem for us because, as I mentioned before, at that time it was believed that you shouldn't bathe more than once a week, or wash your hair more frequently than about every three weeks for fear of washing the natural oils out of your skin and hair.

Richard was much more daring than I was, and climbed higher up trees than I dared. About half a mile from where we lived, a stream ran under the town in a tunnel about 4ft in diameter and a quarter of a mile long. To get to its entrance, it was necessary to climb down a steep embankment. Richard accomplished that more easily than I did. Once by the stream, when we bent down, it was just possible to see daylight at the far end of the tunnel. I wanted to crawl through it with Richard, but dared not do so. But he dared. 'I'm going!' he said and, straddling the stream with a leg on either side of the tunnel, he prepared to depart, whereupon I became angry in an effort to hold him back and, I suppose, make him behave like me. 'I'm older than you,' I said. 'What if someone catches you or you get stuck. Mum and Dad will be furious!' But he didn't care about what I said, and disappeared into the tunnel, quickly becoming smaller and smaller until he was merely a small black shadow against the daylight at its opposite end. I was furious when he came back about thirty minutes later. 'Look at your boots!' I snapped. 'They're scuffed and wet. Don't blame me if you cop it when we get home.' On seeing his boots, Mum got hold of him by the ear, and dragged him into the kitchen and gave him a good telling off, which may sound harsh, but was against a background of him kicking his way through his boots and tearing his trousers so often that Mum arranged a regular order on his behalf for trousers from Devonshires, the men and boys' draper's shop in the parade of shops on the opposite side of the road to our shop. For the same reason, a regular order for boots was placed at Batas, the shoe shop in the High Road, about a mile from where we lived.

★★★

My best friend at that time was a boy named Lawrence Osborne, who was about my age, and whom I had met when we were playing on the piles of bricks at the time the street shelters were being built.

Shortly after we met, he took me to his home, a 1920s semi-detached house in a side road about 200 yards behind the shop. The hall of the house was a soulless grey-brown colour, as was the rest of the house. Later I learnt that his parents were musicians who lived for their music and weren't bothered about such things. As Lawrence led me towards the room at the back of the house, I was aware on my left of a stringed musical instrument being played behind the closed door of the front room. I had no idea what instrument it was, as the only stringed instrument I knew of was Mum's violin. But I was aware that it had a deeper note than that.

'My mother!' Lawrence explained, flicking his head of thick black, curly hair towards the door the sound was coming from. 'She's practising the cello. But we won't bother her. She won't even know we're here. She's almost deaf.'

It turned out that his parents played in various orchestras such as the London Symphony Orchestra. His mother, who I met briefly later that morning, was a thin, pale, colourless wisp of a woman who, because she was almost totally deaf, watched my lips rather than my eyes as I spoke to her.

In contrast to his mother, Lawrence's father was a rotund, swarthy little man with fierce, bulging black eyes and wavy black hair, all of which suggested to my young mind that he could be Mexican. He played the trumpet, and I wondered if his eyes bulged as a result of the pressure required to blow into it. It didn't take a genius to guess from which of his parents Lawrence inherited his looks. With his black hair and almost black eyes, he was a small replica of his father.

I saw Mr Osborne only very occasionally, as he had been conscripted into the air force at the beginning of the war and was currently serving as a sergeant in the RAF regimental band. He seemed to thrive on messages of doom and imminent national disaster, and was full of tales about the expected invasion. The first time I met him he asked me, 'How's your father getting on with being a policeman?' When I had finished telling him, he looked away, then looking back at me he said, his eyes bulging fiercely, 'What does he think about the war? A bad business, if ever there was one. It's wrecked my career.' With a scowl, he shook his head in exactly the same way as Lawrence had done when I first entered their home; then, as if he had an itch on the top of his head, he ran his fat little fingers through his hair.

Lawrence's grandparents lived across the street from his home, and on one occasion I visited them with him. Apart from his grandparents, who I remember as two small, bustling, elderly people who welcomed us warmly into their home, my main memory of the visit is of a copy of a famous painting on the wall of their hall. The subject of the painting was the boyhood of Sir Walter Raleigh. In the painting, the future Sir Walter is depicted sitting on the ground with his knees clasped in front of him, as he listens with rapt attention to an old seafarer, who is pointing across the sea, telling the future Sir Walter about the call of the sea and faraway lands beyond the horizon. Although I had no idea of it at the time, some years later, I realised that that picture summed up my own wish for a life of adventure, and that it contributed to my choice of career.

Among Lawrence's toys was a fine collection of lead soldiers, and while his mum practised the cello in the front room, Lawrence and I played in a little world of our own in front of the French windows in the back room. We arranged the soldiers in lines facing one another on the floor and for several hours fought battles with them. Among them were guardsmen in red tunics, black trousers, with busbies on their heads, and rifles raised horizontally in the firing position; Native Americans in full headdress with white feathers flowing down their backs like horses' manes and tomahawks raised at the ready; soldiers in khaki with weapons in various firing positions; and soldiers on horseback, dressed in red tunics and black trousers with white helmets on their heads and lances that pointed up towards the sky in their hands.

In the summer, Lawrence and I played in his garden, which, in keeping with the state of the house, was neglected and overgrown and like a small suburban jungle. It was a super place for boys to play in. We formed a gang and made our headquarters on a tiny platform we constructed from bits of wood, halfway up a large willow tree at the back of the garden. It was our secret place. The only other members of our gang were our dogs: Bingo, my black and white spaniel, and Peter, Lawrence's black and brown Airedale. On several occasions, we tried to lift Bingo up onto the platform but, although he was patient and allowed us to put a sling under his belly, he proved to be too heavy for us to winch up using a length of domestic washing line slung over a branch of the tree as a pulley.

Later in the year we found a set of old pram wheels, and made a dogcart and harnessed Bingo to it in the expectation that he would pull us about, but he flatly refused to do so.

★★★

Sometimes, Richard invited me to play with his friends. His best friend was a boy named Christopher Young. I liked to go to Christopher's home. Usually, when I went his parents were at work. His father was a very tall man with big, long feet, who I rarely saw as he left early for work each weekday morning. Chris' mother was the personal assistant of Firth Shephard, the well-known theatre impresario, and was also usually away at work when I visited. When they were out, the home was looked after by Chris's two elderly grandmas. To me, Grandma Young seemed to be very old, which was a reasonable assumption as in retrospect I think she was probably aged about 90. The skin on her face was like crumpled white velvet. The part of her face beneath her nose seemed to have collapsed as a result of her teeth having decayed and fallen out a long time ago. A few white strands of hair remained curled up on her otherwise bald scalp. She did very little but sit for most of the day at the downstairs front window, with one of the two house cats on her lap, while looking out to see who was going up and down the street. Although she didn't say much, she always gave me a friendly, toothless grin when I called with Richard to collect Chris, and go up to the park to climb trees, or fly a kite that had been made from balsa wood and tissue paper by a boy named Alan, who was older than us, and went to the local grammar school.

In contrast with Grandma Young, Grandma Saville, Mrs Young's mother, was a small dynamo of a woman, with a mop of iron-grey hair cut short back and sides. She rushed around like a ferret, cleaning the house, cooking for the family, and doing a local round for the Prudential Insurance Company; and because she was so busy, she gave me the impression of having little time for us boys.

# 7

# AN AEROPLANE IS SHOT DOWN

One day, Dad told Richard and me that a German aeroplane had been shot down and crashed in a ball of fire close to a hedge on a smallholding that had been bequeathed to him by his father, Grandpa Model. It was in the tiny hamlet of Dunton, close to the village of Laindon in Essex, approximately 30 miles to the east of London.

'One of the crew was burned to death, poor devil. The other sustained a broken leg and couldn't move very far,' Dad said. 'Old Gibson, the tenant farmer, went out with a pitchfork and arrested him, and guarded him until the army came and took him away.'

It was the type of story that boys like Richard and I revelled in.

'Can I go and see the plane? I asked Dad eagerly.

I cannot remember how we got there – whether it was by train to Laindon, or if we still had enough petrol to go by car, but I very clearly remember the scene when we got there.

First, we went to see Mr Gibson, a John Bull of a man, large and rotund with legs clad in leather gaiters, and very firmly planted on the floor of the farmhouse kitchen. The latter was a neglected, sparsely furnished room, except for a large, dark mahogany table in its centre. As usual, Mr Gibson was wearing a trilby hat and was unshaven, with a day or two's growth of beard on his face. He feared Dad's visits, as they were connected in his mind with the requirement to pay several months of unpaid rent.

'How are things?' Dad asked, reluctantly shaking the hand Mr Gibson offered him. 'And by the way, have you got the rent?'

'All right,' Mr Gibson replied grudgingly. 'You know about that Jerry plane that crashed in the big field?'

'I've brought my boys to see it,' Dad said, nodding towards Richard and me.

Mr Gibson produced a pile of grubby bank notes, and handed them to Dad, who took them, counted them individually on the table, then stuffed them into the inside pocket of his jacket. Afterwards, Dad, Richard and I left the house and trudged over to the far side of the nearest field, which was bounded by a hedge in which several large trees were growing. Close to the hedge were the burnt-out remains of the plane, covering an area about the size of a tennis court. It was a scene of utter destruction. The earth within the area was scorched and covered in piles of thick grey cinders tinged with black. Protruding beyond them on the left were the remains of one of the wings of the plane, its upper side clearly marked with a black German cross. The tail and middle part of the fuselage of the aircraft had gone up in the flames, but slightly ahead and to our right were the twisted remains of the forward part of cockpit. Foremost among them was what was left of the dashboard, with several dials still on it.

Carefully, Richard and I picked our way towards the dials.

'Can I have one of them?' I asked Dad.

The flames had scalded and weakened the metal remains of the plane, and with Dad's help, we loosened and eventually freed two of the dials. If I remember correctly, I had an altimeter. Richard had a speedometer.

Afterwards, we boys searched through the cinders to see if we could find any remains of the man who had been burnt to death. I can only surmise the horror I would have felt if we had found the remains of a human arm, but thankfully, we didn't find any such remnants.

When we had finished looking at the plane, we carried the dials back to the farmhouse, where Mr Gibson gave each of us a brown paper bag to put them in. Then, we made our way down the lane to the cottage in which Dad's father, Grandpa Model, lived with his wife Mabel on a piece of land that was part of the farm.

Despite many visits, as we approached the cottage, I noticed for the first time just how poor and run down it was. It seemed to grow out of the ground. Its walls – made of scorched red brick – bulged in several places, and its tiled roof was higgledy-piggledy and went up and down like a low swell on the sea. The front door was made of cheap, tongue-and-groove planking and was painted racing-car green. Its only toilet was a smelly, wooden privy over a cesspit a few yards behind the back door.

Grandpa opened the front door and greeted us in a gruff old man's well-meaning way. Although I was young,

I was experienced enough to appreciate that he was a fine-looking, upright elderly man with a large white walrus moustache and a mop of soft white hair that looked like candyfloss. His boots were so highly polished that you could see your face in them. I loved Grandpa. When I was a baby, he liked to hold me in the crook of his arm and feed me a tiny drop of port that, apparently, I gulped down as it was sweet.

How looks can deceive! My fine-looking elderly Grandpa had a dark past. I would later learn that you cannot judge a person's character by their face, and that a person with a kind-looking face may have a wolf's heart, while someone with a beaten up-looking face may have a heart of gold. But I didn't know about such things when we visited Grandpa that day, and did not appreciate that my fine-looking old Catholic Grandpa was a repentant sinner, trying to make amends for a life of heavy drinking, fast living and womanising that had resulted in several children born out of wedlock, and that on at least two occasions he had been divorced by distraught wives. I don't know if Dad knew about Grandpa's past, as we never discussed it, but if he did, I can only surmise that he would have been both embarrassed and disgusted.

Inside, the cottage was primitive. Downstairs, it consisted of only one room dominated at its far end by a large, old-fashioned, black kitchen range on which a kettle was always boiling. I sat at the dining table that was up against a wall and, while Dad and Grandpa talked, I looked round the room, and drank the cup of tea and ate the biscuits that Mabel offered me from a wooden biscuit barrel. For most of our visit, Mabel stood motionless beside the table, never uttering a word, but instead peeping out from behind her glasses. She was a thin broomstick of an old lady, wearing a floral apron over an old blue dress that was too large for her, and from which the hem hung unevenly.

Twenty years previously she had met Grandpa when she was a novice nun in a nursing order. Grandpa had had one of the early successful colostomies for cancer of the bowel. The remaining lower end of his bowel had been diverted and brought out through his abdominal wall, where it discharged into a bag. Mabel had nursed him at home after the surgery, and it wasn't long before he came to rely on her, and one thing led to another and she left the nursing order of nuns and married him.

The cottage had only recently been supplied with electricity, and a single unlit light bulb hung from a wire in the centre of the ceiling. Everywhere, there was evidence of the Catholic faith. A small round porcelain relief of a pope's head hung from either side of the kitchen range. On the wall above me, as I sat at the table, was a large, 3ft-long wooden relief of the Last Supper, carved, as I would later appreciate, in the manner of the famous painting by Leonardo da Vinci. Hanging on the opposite wall was a small wooden crucifix from which the dead Christ hung, his knee flexed by the weight of his body.

Below the crucifix was an old leather-covered chaise longue on which Grandpa napped in the afternoon. A spring protruded from a hole in its middle. The arguments over the hole and the spring were a microcosm of the way Grandpa and Dad irritated one another. Before he lay down, Grandpa covered the hole with a wad of old newspapers, which I remember to this day were copies of the *Daily Express* – other pages of which he tore up and used as toilet paper in the privy. Dad thought Grandpa was mean, and that the chaise longue should be re-covered. Grandpa agreed when Dad suggested it to him during the course of each of our visits, but ignored it as soon as we had gone. And so it went on. Each time Dad saw the hole there was an argument. They also argued about politics and their different views of the world. Dad was a socialist at that time, and Grandpa a Conservative.

Whereas Dad, Mabel, Richard and I drank our tea from a cup, Grandpa sat in his armchair and poured it into his saucer, and after placing the cup on a corner of the table, lifted the saucer up to his mouth with both hands and, with loud sucking sounds, sucked up the tea. I knew what Mum would have said on the way home if she had been with us: 'Don't ever let me catch you doing that!'

On the way home, Dad told us that when he was young, he and his little sister, my Aunty Lilly, had lived with Grandpa in a large house overlooking Wanstead Flats, and that Grandpa had been rich and had owned a couple of horses and traps. What Dad didn't tell us was what had happened to Grandpa's money. I was a man aged about 25 before I found out that, like many people, before the First World War Grandpa had invested heavily in Russian railways and had lost almost all his money when the communists nationalised them when they took over Russia in 1917.

At home that night when Mum and I were alone in the kitchen, she told me that Dad had had an unhappy childhood:

His mother died shortly after the birth of your Aunty Lilly, and your Grandpa tried to rear him and his brothers on his own, and the baby Lilly with the aid of a series of

housekeepers. Subsequently, he married one of the housekeepers. Your Dad told me that his father probably loved
him and his brothers and Lilly, but he didn't know how to
express it or how to bring them up. He's a Victorian, and
believed in harsh discipline and in the saying 'spare the rod
and spoil the child', so frequently he beat the boys with
horse reins when they were naughty, or did not quite do
what he wanted of them. Dad's brothers left home as soon
as they could, and only see their father when they want
money from him, and not at all now as he hasn't got any.

Your father's the only one who's kept in contact with
him or sees him. Your Dad was good at school and wanted
to be an historian. He hasn't told you, but I can tell you he
was also good at football and cricket, and as a schoolboy
had trials for Essex at cricket and West Ham for football.
But Grandpa wasn't interested in things like that, and
would not allow your Dad to take up an offer to train with
the Essex cricket team. He was an old-fashioned man who
had come to England from Germany when he was little
more than a boy in order to escape conscription into the
Kaiser's army, or perhaps escape the clutches of a girl who
might have been going to have his baby. He had no idea of
the value of education, and that once you've got it, no one
can take it away from you. He thinks everyone should earn
a living and bring home a wage packet from as early an
age as possible and so, despite the fact that he was wealthy
at that time and, if he wanted, could have afforded for your
Dad to go to university, he took him away from school
as soon as he was 14 and set him to work looking after
the farm. Your Dad hated it. That's why he's so keen for
you and Richard to do well at school. He wants you to
have the chances he didn't have. He had to get up at five

o'clock in the morning to milk the cows and have the milk ready for collection at eight o'clock. And then, he had to do everything on the farm, cutting hedges, putting in fences and things like that.

He did it for five years, but when the General Strike occurred in 1926, he saw his chance to get away. He went up to London and drove a bus. In a way, I suppose, you could say he was a strike breaker. Anyway, when the strike was over, work was difficult to get. There were lots of unemployed people, and lots of men who had been soldiers during the war and were looking for work. Your Dad was good-looking and got the only job he could, as an apprentice with Teazy-Weazy, the famous West End hairdresser. So that's how he came to be a hairdresser when really he wanted to be a historian.

I was confused and shocked. How could my fine-looking old Grandpa, whom I loved, and who was so upright and looked so handsome, have been such an awful man when he was young? It didn't seem possible to my young mind. He looked so benign with his old man's white hair and white moustache.

My thoughts were interrupted by Mum who, continuing her conversation about Dad, smiled and said, 'Your Dad's so handsome that often I wonder why he married a plump, plain woman like me.'

Her comments made me smile quietly to myself. I knew why Dad married her! I went over to her and cuddled up against her. She felt soft and warm and mumsy and oozed love, and I felt very safe and secure with her. Dad might have had all the good looks of a matinee film star, but now that I knew how hard and frustrating his life had been, although I couldn't have expressed it at the time, instinctively I appreciated that Mum was a natural home for his doubts and frustrations, just as she was for mine. She might criticise and be angry with me at times, but for as long as she lived, she empathised with me during the times in my life when I had troubles – and believe me, I had plenty!

Dad being a hairdresser had its advantages so far as Richard, Mum and I were concerned. He cut the hair of all three of us, and even trimmed Bingo's fur at the beginning of each summer. For the whole of the time that I lived at home, which was until I was an adult, I never went to a barbers; indeed if I had, I would not have known what to ask for.

The day after the visit to the farm, the dial I had obtained from the plane earned me a lot of respect among my friends on the streets.

'Cor! Where'd you get that?' John Curtis asked.

A group of other boys I played with in the Old Field also wanted to know how I got it. I told them that my Dad owned a farm in Essex, and that a German bomber had been brought down on it, and that earned me even more respect.

★★★

One of the strongest messages I got from my parents, particularly Mum, was about the need to work hard. Without doubt, Mum was a workaholic. To be a business-owner, a wife and a mother of two boys required a great deal of energy and considerable determination. Twice a week a lady named Mrs Pink came to help with cleaning the flat, but that didn't prevent Mum from bustling around in a smock for the first two hours of the day with a duster and a wash leather in her hand. Inevitably, the room I shared with Richard came within the orbit of her attention. We liked having our toys spread out on the floor and our clothes slung over the back of a chair but within a few minutes she would whirl through the room and reduce it to looking as clean and spartan as a barrack room.

Every day from Monday to Friday she cleaned both the insides and outsides of the windows at the front of the flat. As they were over the shop and about 15ft above the ground, she was obliged to do them from the inside. The bottom windows were easy enough to get at, but the small top ones were high up and difficult to clean, and the only way she could do it was by getting up onto the inside windowsill and pressing herself against the glass before reaching out as far as she could through the window that opened. Dad asked her repeatedly not to do it, but she would not listen. The neighbours thought it was a huge joke, and on one occasion a man named Mr Jones, who lived in a house directly opposite the shop, said to his wife, 'There's only one thing worse than you scrubbing our bloody front doorstep every day, and that's that woman over there cleaning her bloody windows each morning!'

At half past ten, by which time the place looked as if it had been spring cleaned, Mum had a bath and went down to the shop, which had been opened at nine o'clock by a young lady named Freda Wrench, one of the two assistants who helped Mum in the shop. Dad helped by collecting goods from the warehouses with which Mum dealt and if I wasn't at school, I would often accompany him. Mum had a knack with people, and the ladies who worked for her, such as Freda and Mrs Gray, became friends and part of our lives. It was as if there was blood between us; we knew their families and partook of their lives. Eventually, Freda married a good-humoured man named Ron, and after the war the two of them emigrated to Australia but kept in contact with us for many years.

Like many small traders, Mum's business relied to a large degree on the personal service she offered and the loyalty it engendered. She knew many of her customers personally. Some came in for a chat as they were passing by, rather than to buy anything. She listened to their troubles and shared their joys and sorrows long before the idea of counselling was developed. One lady named Mrs Guthrie came in almost every Monday afternoon, and I knew her well. As I usually went into the shop after school to find out if there were any errands to run, and to ask if I might have a slice of bread and dripping when I went upstairs, I often met Mrs Guthrie, who would be sitting having a cup of tea with Mum. She was from Yorkshire and referred to her daughter as 'Our Joyce'. Joyce was the same age as me, and like me, was a pupil at Wembley House School. Each year, Richard and I went to her home in a nearby street for her birthday party and, along with a dozen or so other kids, played games such as charades, musical chairs and pin the tail on the donkey, and ate cakes and jelly and blancmange. In their front room, the Guthries had a pianola, an upright piano that, when peddled, played music automatically. Inside it was an embossed roll of paper that instructed it to play musical notes in perfect order, so that even someone as unmusical as me could appear to play the piano as well as a professional. Pianolas were common in those days but are rare now, as most people have digital ways of reproducing music.

Every week, salesmen from various wholesalers called to see if Mum wanted any stock for the shop. Most of them were highly respectable men and women. Mr Jones was an immaculately dressed middle-aged man from a wholesaler named Pawson and Leafs, which had been bombed out and forced to move from its original premises adjacent to St Paul's Cathedral. Dressed in a three-piece suit and a white shirt with a detachable stiff white collar, Mr Jones spoke in a soft confidential voice and jotted down orders in an order book

By contrast, Mrs MacMichael was a large, bosomy woman with a mass of grey hair piled up on the front of her head like a wave about to break over the deck of a ship. Usually when I saw her, she was sitting behind the counter drinking tea with Mum and warming herself by the electric fire.

Mrs Lewis was a small Jewish woman with sad black eyes that had large, baggy pouches under them. She sold Mum shiny patent-leather handbags, which her husband made at home as their factory had been destroyed in the bombing. I liked Mrs Lewis because she was friendly and called me 'Darling', and because she had long, painted, red fingernails that I thought were very feminine. I also liked her son Henry, who, when we visited their home in Ealing, showed me the collection of birds' eggs he had purchased and kept in trays in a specially constructed chest of drawers. He had a beautiful sister named Josie. When Mrs Ferris saw Josie's face and long black tresses, she said, 'What a beautiful child!' I agreed. I was secretly in love

with Josie but was shy and kept my feelings to myself for
fear of being rebuffed.

# 8

# AMERICA RELUCTANTLY JOINS THE WAR

Christmas 1941 was a difficult time. The Germans' advance had taken them to the gates of Moscow. On 8 December I heard on the radio that on the previous day the Japanese had bombed Pearl Harbor and had sunk several American battleships. The American Senate responded by declaring war on Japan following a speech by President Roosevelt in which he referred to the day on which the bombing occurred as 'a day of infamy'.

Also on 8 December, the Japanese invaded the British territory of Malaya. In Wembley, the boys I played with in the Old Field said, 'The Japs are boss-eyed. They all wear glasses and can't see properly! They'll never be able to hit their targets!'

How wrong they were! On 10 December Japanese torpedo planes sank two British capital ships, the battleship HMS *Prince of Wales* and the battlecruiser HMS *Repulse*, off the coast of Malaya with the loss of more than 900 British lives. The sinkings left me confused. If the Japanese couldn't see properly, how could they so easily have sunk two of our most famous warships? In the Atlantic, German U-boats were sinking ever-greater numbers of Allied merchant ships, causing large reductions in the supply of goods reaching Britain. In response to all this, my friends said, 'There is only one good Jap or German, and that's a dead Jap or German.'

Rationing was at its height. In the shops, goods were scarce and difficult to come by. Chocolates, alcoholic drinks such as gin, and even turkeys were in short supply. Soap was so scarce that Mum bought a soap saver, a wire cage in which pieces of soap that were too small to use were placed and shaken in water to make it soapy enough to wash up in. A policy of 'make do and mend' was introduced by the government, encouraging housewives to be stylish yet frugal and mend and reuse old clothes.

During the week before Christmas, Richard and I were kept busy making paper chains from packets of coloured strips of paper that Mum managed to buy. We made yards and yards of them, and Dad strung them diagonally from the wall to the light in the middle of the kitchen, and then onto the wall on the opposite side of the room, and later, in the front room. In keeping with make do and mend, some people made their paper chains from strips of newspaper.

Most toys that were available were expensive and shoddily made and so, although Richard and I found our

Christmas stockings full of goodies when we got up in the small hours of Christmas morning, there was a dearth of toys. The main gifts we received were National Savings Books with which to save part of our weekly wages of 6d. To encourage us, Mum started us off with four stamps in each of our books. When we had saved 2s 6d, we went to the post office and proudly bought a stamp that we equally proudly stuck into our books. The books gave us a sense of ownership and, combined with the privations of the war, instilled in me the lifelong habit of saving and sense of thrift that, later in my life, expressed itself in the belief that I should not buy anything I could not pay for immediately.

On 16 February 1942, I heard on the radio that on the previous day the British fortress of Singapore had surrendered to the Japanese. I was old enough to understand the implications of that, and realised it was a terrible defeat. The stories I heard about it – that may or may not have been true – were that, under cover of the Malayan jungle, the Japanese were able to advance south from the foothold they had established in northern Malaya and, using bicycles and other means of transport, had travelled along paths and minor roads that allowed them to sidestep Allied forces that had been sent to oppose them. Eventually they arrived at the island of Singapore, which was thought to be impregnable to attack by sea, but had few defences against the overland route used by the Japanese. After resisting for as long as they could, some 80,000 British, Indian and Australian soldiers were taken prisoner, and subsequently treated atrociously, many dying of starvation, overwork, beatings and infections such as malaria. It was the largest surrender of British,

Commonwealth and Empire troops ever recorded, and was described by Mr Churchill as the 'worst disaster' and 'largest capitulation' in British military history.

★★★

Early in 1942, American and Commonwealth soldiers and airmen began to arrive in Britain in preparation for the invasion of Europe and freeing of its people from the Nazi yoke. The Americans were a boon to Richard and me. Many of them were young, only a dozen or so years older than we were. I was told that they had received instructions about how to deal with the 'natives', and in general they were very friendly and polite. They looked upon us as 'cute'. Unlike British and Commonwealth troops, who wore thick khaki battledress, the Americans wore uniforms that looked like khaki two-piece suits. Also, unlike the grey-blue uniforms of the RAF, airmen of the US Eighth Air Force, which was stationed in the part of the country in which we lived, wore khaki uniforms, similar to those of the US Army. They had food of a type that Richard and I couldn't remember ever having tasted, such as ice cream and bananas. When we saw an American serviceman, we would go up to him and say, 'Got any gum, Chum?' and, as like as not, many of them gave us a piece of chewing gum or occasionally a bar of chocolate, sometimes adding something such as, 'OK Limey kids. Here you are!'

Not everyone welcomed the Americans. They were strangers from the land of cowboys and Hollywood. They were well mannered, well dressed and better paid than British servicemen. They had a surfeit of chocolates, cigars and cigarettes, and even nylon stockings, and were attractive to many English women. So, it was not surprising that some English people said that they were 'overpaid, oversexed and over here'. However, the lives of many of them were tragically short. The US Air Force bombed Germany by day, and the RAF bombed it by night. Both suffered horrendous casualties. Several officers of the Eighth Air Force joined Dad's golf club and told him that the expectation of life for many US airmen was just a few weeks or months.

Not all the soldiers assembling in Britain were as polite or as friendly as the Americans. One afternoon, Richard and I went by Underground train with Mum and Dad to see a film in Leicester Square, and saw two kilted soldiers give a smart salute to an officer who was walking by. As soon as he had passed, they turned their backs to him, lifted their kilts, and in a show of defiance, thrust their backsides towards his disappearing figure.

A few days later, a soldier from Canada phoned Mum and Dad, and shortly afterwards came to visit us in our home above the shop. He arrived with a guitar and a box of greatly appreciated chocolates. Cousin Syd, as I was told to call him, was a softly spoken dark-haired young man wearing khaki battledress similar to that worn by British soldiers, except for flashes on his shoulders saying 'Canada'. He was a distant relative of Uncle Mark, Aunty Rose's husband, and told us that he lived in Winnipeg, and that before the war he had been a fir trapper, which in my imagination prompted visions of dark Canadian pine forests and grizzly bears. So, I asked him, 'Have you ever trapped a grizzly bear?' He smiled and said, 'No, Douglas. I've seen a few, but adult grizzlies are very tall and very strong and mighty dangerous, and so we give them a wide berth. Mostly we trap animals such as fox, beaver, muskrat and lynx.'

After tea, he took up his guitar and entertained us by singing cowboy songs and chatting with us until it was time to return to his unit.

★★★

Later in the spring of 1942, Mum and Dad, Richard and I visited Grandpa Model with the intention of going on later to see Mum's family in the small nearby town of Laindon. As usual at Grandpa Model's, lunch consisted of two mean little pieces of cold roast lamb and a few runner beans and mashed potatoes grown in his vegetable garden. Afterwards, Richard and I ventured through the door to the right of the kitchen range. Even before the door was fully opened, we saw that we were entering an old cow-shed that was joined to the cottage. Its roof was about 9 or 10ft above our heads and, like its walls, it had been white-washed long ago. Dust and grime abounded everywhere and covered the white of the walls in a thin grey film. Cobwebs hung from the beams supporting the roof, from cracks and crevices on the walls and covered an ancient plough and gardening tools that were heaped against the far wall. Only the nearest part of the floor had been tiled. The rest was impacted earth.

Close to the door was a large, old, chipped, rectangular porcelain kitchen sink standing on two columns of cemented bricks. Next to it was an old iron hand pump of the type seen on village greens, with a handle for pumping water up from a well below. It was the only source of water in the cottage. Beyond the pump was the largest mangle I have ever seen. Mangles have gone now, but in their day they were used for wringing out clothes. Wet clothes fed into one side of Grandpa's mangle would emerge from the other side flat and almost dry, and ready to be hung up on the washing line that straddled part of his well-cared-for vegetable garden.

From Grandpa Model's we went to see Mum's family in Laindon. Goodness knows why Grandpa and Grandma Morris had chosen to move from London to such a rundown place. For me it was epitomised one Sunday afternoon when I was sitting by the window in Grandma's upstairs bedroom, looking out over what passed for a high street. Everywhere was wet and grey. On the opposite side of the road were a few rundown shops and a mishmash of untarred muddy roads and down-at-heel bungalows. Not a soul was to be seen, not even a cat or stray dog. The only sound was the patter of rain hitting the window, and running in rivulets down the glass pane immediately in front of my face.

The two shops that Grandpa Morris had built some twenty years earlier were the only fine shops in the town. Spanning both of them was a large spacious home in which Grandpa and Grandma lived with my Aunty Rose, her husband Mark and their family. The shops had a connecting door between them. One shop was a ladies' outfitters run by Aunty Rose and the other was a men's drapers run by Uncle Mark. I knew the men's shop well. Each time we visited, Uncle Mark allowed Richard and me to buy a couple of pairs of short trousers and shirts at cost price. Almost eighty years later, I can still recall the inside of the shop. It was lined up to the ceiling by shelves containing men's and boys' trousers, shirts and underwear that gave off a wonderful smell of new clothes mixed with mothballs.

Apart from Grandpa, Grandma, Aunty Rose and Uncle Mark, the home above the shops was sufficiently large to also have accommodated Aunty and Uncle's four children – Gordon, Maurice, George, and their sister Helen, all of whom had moved out or were presently living away. The three boys were in the armed forces. Gordon was a captain in the army and was about to be seconded to the Indian Army. Maurice was a major in the army, and George was a sergeant in the RAF. Helen had been married for about a year, and a few days previously had given birth to a baby boy who had been named Geoffrey.

Aunty Rose was in tears when she answered the door to let us in. After exchanging a few words with Mum and Dad, Dad turned to Richard and me, and said, 'Boys, go back to the car, and stay there until we come out to get you.'

As instructed, Richard and I retired to the car and sat in the back, fidgeting and waiting for almost two hours. Mum's eyes were red from crying when she and Dad eventually emerged. Dad had a stern look on his face, as if he was trying to control his emotions.

'It's terrible,' Mum said, when they had seated themselves in the front of the car. Then, addressing us, she said, 'You know your cousin Helen had a little boy five days ago? Well, this morning, for some reason that isn't clear, she died suddenly of what is called milk fever.' She began to cry again, but stopped and blew her nose.

'I think we should go home,' Dad said quietly. 'No good hanging around here.'

'She was such a beautiful young woman,' Mum said, as the car pulled away from the curb. 'I don't understand how anyone so young and fit could die so suddenly after having a baby. There were no complications when the baby was born. Goodness knows who will look after the poor little boy. Lewis can hardly do it.'

Lewis was Helen's husband. He and Helen had visited our home on a couple of occasions. He owned a small factory making electrical parts for the war effort. Before the war, the factory had made lead soldiers and other toys. He still had the moulds for making the soldiers, and each time he visited us, he brought Richard and me a dozen or so unpainted lead soldiers in various poses.

Mum was correct; Lewis said he could not look after the baby. He was so upset and heartbroken by the death of his wife that he wanted only one thing – to die – and within a few days he signed up with the RAF. He requested to be trained as an aircraft tail gunner in the knowledge that tail gunners had a high mortality rate and a low life expectancy. Two or three months later his plane was shot down over the English Channel and he was drowned.

His orphaned son, Geoffrey, was adopted and brought up by Aunty Rose, who doted on him.

# 9

# ABUSE

In July 1942 the Germans began an offensive against the city of Stalingrad that eventually would cost them dear and mark a turning point in the war.

In early November of the same year we learnt that in North Africa British and Commonwealth soldiers led by a general we had not heard much of, named Montgomery, had won a great victory over Rommel's Afrika Korps at a place near the Egyptian border named El-Alamein. The victory at the Battle of El-Alamein was the beginning of the end of the war in North Africa, and Mr Churchill was so delighted that he ordered the church bells to be rung in Britain for the first time since hostilities had begun. In one of his speeches, he said, 'Now, this is not the end, it is not even the beginning of the end. But it is, perhaps, the end of the beginning.'

★★★

By the summer of 1942, the bombing of Britain had become intermittent and there were gaps of several weeks between air raids. As a result, people became complacent, going back to an almost pre-war way of living. They stopped sleeping in their shelters, and started to go to the cinema and the theatre again. On Saturday mornings, the girls from next door, Richard and I and went to the children's matinee at the local Odeon. I loved the stuffy, close smell of the cinema, and sitting in the darkness, I gave myself up to the story, and along with several hundred other kids, cheered Don Winslow, the captain of an American destroyer, as he sank the enemy without any apparent effort. Others I cheered in the darkness were the Lone Ranger and his faithful Native American companion Tonto; Roy Rogers and his faithful horse Trigger; and Hopalong Cassidy, the relaxed cowboy who enforced the law. I booed the Bowery Boys and any gangsters who appeared. Afterwards, when the films were over, we played cops and robbers and cowboys and Indians among the shop fronts and front gardens we passed on our way home.

One Saturday morning Richard was unwell and unable to accompany me to the cinema, so afterwards I made my way home on my own. Halfway along Wembley High Road, I turned left and went down several flights of steps between two shops. The steps led to a backstreet and a short cut home. Suddenly, as I was making my way along the backstreet I was accosted by a boy about five or six years older than me. He towered over me, a big, strong, rough-looking fellow with short and curly brown hair and a surly face. Taking me by the arm, he pushed me into an alleyway between two houses and pinned me against a wooden fence.

'Look at this!' he said. 'It's strong! I want you to remember it.' He pulled open the fly of his trousers. 'Here! Look at this!' he said. 'Run your finger along it!'

He took hold of my right hand and squeezed it as hard as he could. I was frightened and winced with pain and, wondering if I would ever get away, did as he bid me.

He watched, and seemingly satisfied, said, 'Get going! And remember, there'll be trouble if you ever tell anyone. I know where you live, and I'll beat you senseless if you tell.'

He released me and I hurried away. I didn't tell anyone about it until writing this. It was the only time I was bullied or abused.

Forty years later I recognised my abuser on a packed London Underground train, travelling in the rush hour from the centre of London to Harrow where, while I was doing a postgraduate course, I was staying with my mother in the house to which she had retired from the shop. The train was so full that the passengers were packed in cheek by jowl, and my abuser and I were separated by only a couple of other passengers. Like me, he was strap-hanging, steadying himself against the motion of the train by holding on with his left arm to a leather strap that was hanging from a metal bar attached to the roof of the carriage. I could see only his upper half, and that he was wearing a cheap-looking grey overcoat that seemed to be too big for him. He was unshaven and had an angry look on his face, which I suspected was present for most of the time, and from his appearance I surmised that he had probably not been very successful. The way he was staring straight ahead with only part of his face visible to me for most of the time made me wonder if he had recognised me. As

I watched, I felt myself becoming angry and angrier. I despised him. I hated him. I wanted revenge. I wanted to harm him. He deserved a thrashing, and I felt I was just the man to deliver it, as I was considerably bigger than he was and, in my anger, judged that it would not be very difficult. I thought about following him when he got off the train. But although I relished the idea of what I might do to him, something deep inside me told me that it was a preposterous idea. After all, I had all but forgotten the incident until this moment, and when all was said and done, he hadn't done me any permanent harm. Nonetheless, it was tempting to contemplate what I might have done, and I enjoyed the thought of it until we were nearly at the next station, when I was jolted from my thoughts by the slowing of the train. We were nearly at Wembley, close to my childhood home and the place where he had abused me. A moment later the train drew to a stop, the doors opened, and I watched as he alighted onto the platform. Within a few seconds, he had gone.

***

Returning to the war, later in the summer of 1942, Richard and I, aged 7 and 9 respectively, found a new pastime – scouring the gutters of the streets near our home for cigarette ends, which we smoked in pipes we had made in the garage that Dad had converted into a workshop. It was all very clandestine. We knew that what we were doing was forbidden, and if anyone approached when we were searching the gutters, we immediately stopped and pretended to be walking along the road. We made the pipes when Dad wasn't in the garage. They were fashioned from a piece of broomstick that we had hollowed out with a drill. Then we drilled a second, smaller hole at right angles to the first, to take the stem. The stem was made from a short piece of bamboo cane from which we cleared the pith by pushing a piece of wire along its centre. When we estimated that we had gathered enough tobacco to fill the pipes, we went to the Old Field, and sitting among the bushes, puffed away and smoked with considerable satisfaction. If Dad had caught us, he would have given us a good hiding. While smoking like that made us feel grown up and stroked our egos, it also made us dizzy and nauseous if we inhaled too deeply, and so we grew tired of it and eventually decided not to do it anymore.

★★★

One afternoon, during one of the few air raids that occurred at that time in the part of London in which I lived, a German aeroplane was shot at and set on fire. The pilot climbed out of his burning cockpit and parachuted down into the garden of a house about 200 yards from our home. I didn't see it happen, but learnt about it an hour or so later. Apparently, some people who lived nearby wanted to lynch him, but the lady in whose garden he had landed took him into her kitchen and gave him a cup of tea while they waited for the police to come and take him away. 'What else could I do?' she said later. 'He looked so young, only about 18.'

Dad was at the police station when he was brought in and said that, although the young airman accepted that he was a prisoner of war, he stood up straight and, acting with dignity, said that he expected to be treated as a German officer.

★★★

Christmas 1942 was a time of mixed blessings. In Britain, our sweets ration was temporarily increased, while soap was added to the list of items that were rationed. Richard and I were delighted by this, but the grown-ups were not, as each person was limited to either just 2oz of toilet soap or 4oz of household soap per month.

Further afield, in the world at large, the terrible battle for the city of Stalingrad was reaching its climax. When he wasn't on police duty, Dad read the *Daily Telegraph* at breakfast each morning, and it wasn't uncommon for Richard and me to look over his shoulder and see pictures of the contorted frozen bodies of dead German soldiers lying in the snow. What we didn't know, and were not told, was that thousands upon thousands of Russian soldiers had died fighting to keep a small bridgehead of land on the River Volga.

In the agony of its fight for survival, Russia repeatedly appealed to its Western Allies to open a second front in Western Europe to relieve the pressure exerted on it by the attacking Germans. In the side street beside the shop lived the Hood family: Mr and Mrs Hood and their son Robin. They were communists and openly harangued people about the need for a second front. I was friends with Robin and went into their home on several occasions, and remember the darkness of the hall leading in from their front door and the stale smell of body odour in the house. I also remember being in their front room, and Mr

Hood pushing his head close to mine and earnestly telling 9-year-old me that Britain and America were purposely allowing Germany and Russia to fight one another to the death in the hope that both would be too weak to stand up to the Western Allies after the war.

On 31 January 1943, Field Marshal Friedrich Paulus, commander of the German armies at Stalingrad, surrendered to the Russians, although it wasn't until 2 February that most of his troops laid down their arms, and the greatest battle of the war came to an end.

But the war was still far from over.

Apart from the war in Russia, in November 1942 American and Free French forces landed in Morocco and Algeria and, together with the British and Commonwealth Eighth Army advancing from the east, formed a pincer movement that in March 1943 forced Rommel's Afrika Korps and their Italian allies to withdraw from the remaining part of Tunisia they still occupied and, in doing so, forced them to leave Africa for good.

# 10

# AN UNCLE VISITS

Early in 1943, my mother's brother, Uncle Sam, and Aunty Suzie, his wife, came to visit us at our home in Wembley. Uncle Sam was the sort of uncle every boy should have. Whenever he visited, he kept us amused by telling us stories about his adventures during the First World War and about our family on Mum's side.

'Uncle! Tell us a story?' Richard and I asked him as soon as he had settled in his usual armchair just in front of Dad's bookcase in our front room. Dad pulled up a chair when he heard that Uncle was about to tell one of his tales.

Uncle wasn't exactly what you might call good-looking. He was very fat, round and bald, and looked like Humpty Dumpty, the egg that fell off the wall, except for a ring of grey hair flecked with black above his ears that reminded me of the rings around Saturn. He had several chins and when he spoke, they wobbled and began to shake. His voice rasped from years of smoking. But none of that mattered. It was all part of our favourite uncle, Uncle Sam – or Samuel, to give his name in full.

'Which story do you want me to tell?' he asked in a voice like sandpaper. He gave a hoarse laugh, and pushed on the floor with his short, fat little legs to help heave himself into a more comfortable position in his armchair.

'The one about when you were in Aldershot!' Richard and I both cried out.

'You mean when I was in the Glass House in Aldershot?' He laughed again. 'I was the worst soldier the British Army has ever had to contend with. So bad that they wanted to get rid of me, but couldn't. I was a conscript, and they had to take me as they found me.' He chortled and his chins wobbled:

They tried to make a soldier of me and, when they couldn't, they put me in the Glass House, the military prison in Aldershot, and each morning they made me run round and round the parade ground with a rifle held high above my head. After that, using a toothbrush, they made me scrub the two flights of steps leading up to the sergeants' mess. Then, when I'd almost finished, the sergeant would come along in muddy boots, and walk up the steps and kick the bucket over, and say, 'Morris! Get back to the top and start scrubbing the bloody steps again!' And I would have to go back up to the top and start all over again. And again ... and again ... all day long ... But they couldn't make a soldier of me. That was impossible. I just wasn't cut out to be a hero. I didn't want to have anything to do with their war. I wanted to be at home with my family, and work in a local grocery store.

He paused, and coughed and laughed at the same time, and Richard and I said, 'Uncle! What about the one when you were in the front line?'

'Oh, that?' he said, in a voice that might have come from the bottom of a bucket.

Apparently, he had been conscripted into the army when he turned 18, just in time for the Battle of the Somme in the summer of 1916. Uncle continued his story:

Well, the battle had been raging for three weeks by the time I got there, and like everyone else I knew that the first day of the battle had been a terrible tragedy for Britain and the empire, and that a huge number of our men had been killed and wounded [20,000 were killed and 40,000 wounded]. Once I was there, they gave us pep talks and assured us that the barrage of shells they were going to rain down upon the German lines before we went over the top would be so intense that there would be no Germans left alive, and we would be able to stroll into their lines without a shot being fired. But I didn't believe it. I knew I was likely to be killed, and I thought, no way am I going to let that happen to me. So, I'll tell you what I did. On the eve of the day before we were due to go over the top, me and my friend Charlie made a pact to shoot one another in the foot when the whistle blew the following morning for us to go. And that's what we did. The shelling of the German lines had little effect. The Jerry bunkers were so deep that most of our shells couldn't touch them. When the shelling stopped, the Jerrys simply came up and manned their machine guns, and as our boys advanced, they were mown down like flies or blown to bits. Some had their faces shot away, others had their guts ripped open or limbs blown off. I could hear them screaming. I can still hear them screaming at times.

He paused, as if thinking of his dead comrades:

> As the last of them scrambled up out of our trenches, Charlie and I shot one another, and an hour or so later hobbled to the casualty dressing station for help. And who do you think we saw being carried in on a stretcher as we were standing, waiting in the queue … None other than the colonel! He had been badly wounded and was covered in blood, and when he saw me, he said, 'Morris! I know what you did! When I get better I'll have you court-martialled and shot.'
>
> Fortunately for me, the colonel died an hour or so later, God bless him! Later I learnt that of the thousand men in our battalion, only twenty-six were not wounded or killed.

A tear appeared in the corner of each of Uncle's eyes, and he gave a thick phlegmy laugh, looked away and took a deep breath. He was visibly affected by what he had just recounted. Then, as if trying to control and distract himself from his emotions, he reached into his shirt pocket for a box of Player's cigarettes, and took out one and lit it. 'A cigarette cuts the stuff in my throat,' he said gruffly, giving a throaty cough. Collecting himself he continued:

> Now, where was I? Oh, yes, I didn't get sent into any more battles. Instead, because of my wound they put me to peeling spuds for the rest of the war. After the war I got posted to Germany, and was billeted with a German family, and had a thoroughly good time and didn't want to come back.

'Sam, that's enough! You can't keep on boring them with your stories. It'll soon be time for us to go home,' his wife, Aunty Suzie, interrupted him. She was a quiet lady with yellow hair that even I knew was dyed. She hovered round him, keeping her distance from him in case he tried to grab her, in much the same way as Olive Oyl hovered round Popeye in the famous Popeye cartoons.

After they had said goodbye, and we had helped clear up and were preparing to wash up in the kitchen, Mum said to Richard and me, 'You like your Uncle Sam, don't you?' Then, when we nodded affirmatively, she added:

He's loveable, but he's a rogue … he's not a very good example, I'm afraid, and you mustn't believe all he says. He can do bad things at times. What he didn't say was that when he was in Germany he deserted from the army and got taken in by a family who had a daughter. Uncle made her his girlfriend and set up an illegal business importing cigarettes and spirits and selling them to the Germans, as they couldn't get them after the war, as they were defeated and had to pay Britain and its Allies back for causing the war, and as a consequence they didn't have any money. Within a short time your uncle was living a life of luxury and wanted to stay in Germany, but back in England he was already engaged to Aunty Suzie, and when he didn't come home, she went to Grandpa and told him she was going to kill herself if he didn't get your uncle back immediately. Grandpa was so worried that he sent your uncle a telegram ordering him to come back at once to prevent your Aunty Suzie killing herself.

On another occasion Mum told us about the things Uncle got up to when he was a boy.

'He was a bad boy from the time he was a baby,' she said. She continued:

At that time Grandpa owned a fish shop. A piece of fish cost 4*d* in the shop, but out at the back your uncle, aged 4, was selling it for tuppence a piece. Later, when he was aged about 10, he found that steel washers of a certain size could be used instead of coins to obtain chocolate bars from chocolate vending machines and ran a thriving business until the authorities eventually caught up with him. Then, one afternoon when he was aged about 15, Grandma and Grandpa came home to find that the ground floor of their home was completely empty of furniture. On a whim, Sam had sold it to a passing rag-and-bone man. The dining room suite, the sofa and chairs from the drawing room and the kitchen table and chairs had all gone!

Seeing that Richard and I could hardly believe such a story, Mum went on, 'Grandpa wanted to call the police and have Sam arrested, but Grandma protected him and prevailed upon Grandpa not to call them. It's a funny thing.' Mum added after a short pause. 'All of my brothers and sisters were upright, honest citizens, as honest as the day is long, just as Dad and I expect you to be. Your uncle was the only exception.'

But although it was clear that Uncle Sam had done many reprehensible things, because I loved him, they did not affect my opinion of him. To me he was, and remains, the best storyteller I have known and the type of uncle every boy should have.

★★★

It was at about this time, as I began to emerge from the chrysalis-like state of early childhood, that I began to ask questions about the world around me and what I was being taught at school. One day at home, I said to Dad, 'Dad, at school I've been told we are mammals. Does that mean that we are animals like monkeys, cows and dogs?'

'Well, Douglas,' Dad said. 'We are mammals, as you have been taught, and we have bodies that work in a similar way to other animals. But we are very different to all the other animals. There's no other animal that has a brain and a mind like ours that can reason and understand and reflect on the world around us and attempt to change it. So, you see, although we have animal bodies, it is our minds that are special and distinguish us.'

Not long afterwards, I began to question whether I was Jewish or only partly Jewish. I knew that Dad and Grandpa Model were Catholic, and that Mum and her relatives were Jewish, but I was not sure if that meant that I was Jewish, as religion was never discussed at home. So, one day I asked Dad about God and what God was.

'God is love,' Dad said. 'All you have to do is love other people and live a good life.'

But although I tried, I could not understand what Dad meant by saying that God is love, as, although I was young, I knew enough to know that love is a human emotion, something that emanates from inside people, and that it can't possibly be the driving force that created the world and the universe. Nor did Dad's explanation help me understand whether or not I was Jewish or partly Jewish, and if I was Jewish, did that make me different to other people?

You may ask why I was bothered about such matters. The answer is simple: I had picked up the idea of antisemitism and that some people did not like Jews.

The matter came to a head one morning as a lady was walking past the shop at the same time as I was sweeping the pavement. As she passed me, she said in a way that was clearly meant for me to hear, 'Jews are alright, but they smell.' Her words struck me like a blow. They were obviously meant to hurt me, but I did not know how to react. Should I acknowledge what she had said and perhaps reply to her? Instead, I slunk away like a wounded animal. I felt threatened and confused. She had referred to a part of me about which I was unsure. Did Jews smell, and, if so, did I smell? How did she know I might be Jewish or partly Jewish? Was it because of my dark looks, or perhaps because Mum ran a clothes shop, an occupation that seemed to be associated with Jewish people? Whatever it was, it left me feeling insecure and full of doubt and lacking self-confidence.

A few weeks later, another incident occurred that left me feeling equally confused. This time it was at school. It was Easter, the time of the Jewish Passover. A Jewish girl named Naomi, who sat about three desks away from me, volunteered to bring unleavened bread into the class and read to us about it from the Old Testament of the Bible. She was clearly comfortable with her identity, and as I listened to her and ate some of the bread, which of course was matzos, I was seized by conflicting emotions. On the one hand, deep inside me I felt that in a way I did not understand I might be associated with the things she was speaking about. On the other hand, I was aware that I could not acknowledge my feelings because of the unspoken message I had been given at home that discussing religion was taboo. As a result, again I was left feeling confused and in a kind of no man's land.

★★★

One day in March 1943, Dad received the news that Grandpa Model had passed away after a short episode of chest pain. I was in the kitchen when Dad told me, and I was so upset that, as soon as I could, I slunk away and hid in the front room. I needed to be on my own to give expression to my feelings. It was the first time anyone close to me had died. I loved Grandpa, and felt that part of me had been torn away, and I went behind the sofa and sank down in the space between the back of it and the wall, and cried and cried and cried until I could not cry anymore.

# 11

# A SNEAKY BOMBING

The absence of bombing at this time led to people going more freely about their lives than they had been during or after the Blitz.

Wednesday was early closing day in Mum's shop, and one Wednesday shortly after Uncle Sam's visit, Mum and Dad decided to leave Richard and me in the care of Mrs Ferris while they went to the farm that Grandpa Model had given to Dad. Their purpose was to collect the rent from Mr Gibson, the tenant farmer, who, as ever, had once again failed to pay it. During the afternoon while Mum and Dad were away, Richard, Rita and I played in the Ferrises' garden, a small part of which had been given over for the duration of the war to breeding ducks to augment their ration of meat and eggs. I liked watching the ducks waddle about their pen and the way they quacked as they moved, but I hated the sickly smell that pervaded the pen.

Supper was in the Ferrises' morning room, which was almost as big as our front room. After supper, we three children got into our pyjamas in anticipation of a special treat before going to bed. Just after nine o'clock, Mrs Ferris gave each of us a bowl of jelly and blancmange – a treat usually reserved for birthdays and special occasions. We had taken only a few mouthfuls when suddenly our world was filled by the roar of a very loud aeroplane engine. A few seconds later the air-raid siren sounded, but by then a bomb was already on its way towards us.

'Quick, children! Into the Morrison shelter!' Mrs Ferris shouted at us.

In a panic, with thumping hearts and full of fear, we ran from the morning room and dived into the Morrison shelter that Mr Ferris had had erected in their front room. It was like a dining room table made from steel with metal mesh sides, and measured 6ft 6in long, 4ft wide and 2ft 6in high.

Morrison shelter. (Ministry of Information Photo Division Photographer/Imperial War Museums via Getty Images)

At the next moment our world was almost extinguished by a tremendous head-shattering explosion. While that was happening, I could think of only one thing: *please, please dear God, I don't want to die. I want to live. I don't want to die.*

After the explosion we were left wondering what had happened, as our world was enveloped by a silence that is best described as an absence of anything, or perhaps like being in a black vacuum.

For a moment I wondered if I could hear properly; then my senses returned and I became aware of the world around me, and realised that I had survived and was in the Ferrises' Morrison shelter, and that I had a sticky, wet bottom and my pyjamas were wet.

'Oh, golly!' Richard exclaimed.

Apparently, he was experiencing similar sensations to me. A moment later we realised what had happened. In our panic to get into the Morrison shelter, we children had forgotten to put down our plates, and had taken them with us into the shelter and sat on them. As a consequence, our bottoms and pyjamas were wet and sticky with jelly and blancmange.

'I know what's happened!' I said out of devilment that I can only describe as a reaction to the shock of the bombing. 'Rita, have you wet yourself?'

'Be quiet, you awful boy!' she exclaimed angrily.

More drama was about to unfold. In the floor of the Ferrises' hall, the room next to the one containing the Morrison shelter, we found a hole containing a piece of shrapnel about 10in long and weighing about 2lb. It had smashed through the roof of their home, and while still very hot had burned a hole through their first floor and had buried itself in the floor of the hall about 8ft from where we were sitting in the Morrison shelter.

When we were over the shock of the bombing, Mrs Ferris suggested that we take off our wet clothes, wash ourselves and get dressed. The four of us would then go out to find out what had happened and where the bomb had dropped, and to see any damage it might have caused.

As we walked round the side of our home, we were horrified to see that the windows in the front of the shop and our flat above had been blown out and were lying in shards of glass scattered all over the pavement. Inside the window bereft of glass there was a display of half a dozen or so dresses that Mum was hoping to sell. Nearby shops and the homes above them had also had their windows blown out.

Incredulous, we gaped at the devastation.

'Oh, dear God, what will your poor parents say when they get home?' Mrs Ferris muttered.

We guessed that the bomb had exploded in a side street named Douglas Avenue, on the opposite of the main road on which we lived and, as there was little risk of the shop being looted while it was still daylight, we crossed the road and walked towards it. Halfway down on the right were fire engines, ambulances and a crowd of people. As we drew near, we saw that two houses had been completely destroyed, and were lying in heaps of rubble in the hole created by the bomb. On top of the rubble, policemen, firemen, ARP wardens and volunteers from the public were frantically sifting through the rubble, lifting floorboards and throwing furniture and bricks aside as they strove to find any survivors; but none were to be found.

Except for broken windows, no other houses in the street were damaged. Hanging from the walls of the intact two houses immediately adjacent to the destruction was evidence of the lives of the people who were missing. High up on one wall were shreds of green wallpaper where a bathroom had been. Higher still, were the stumps of ceiling rafters that had been torn away in the explosion. On the wall opposite was blue wallpaper with frayed edges where a bedroom had been.

The rescue work continued frantically, but still no survivors were to be found. Then, at about a quarter to eleven, just as it was getting dark, the missing residents of the houses that had been destroyed appeared and pushed their way through the crowd in order to find out what had happened to their homes. By chance, they had taken

Digging out people after an air raid. (The Print Collector/Alamy)

advantage of the lull in the bombing and had gone to a local cinema where, at the time the bomb exploded, they had been watching a film starring Fred Astaire and Ginger Rogers.

Half an hour later, Mum and Dad arrived home, having collected the rent from Mr Gibson. As they drew near, they saw that the windows of the shop and the flat above it had been blown out. Immediately they feared for our safety and, without waiting to inspect the damage, hurried across the side road to the Ferrises' house, where we were waiting to tell them what had happened.

To prevent looting, during the following nights Dad slept on a camp bed in the shop with his police truncheon close by his side until the broken windows had been replaced by sheets of plywood with small glass panes in their centres for customers to look through.

Within our family, Bingo was the member most affected by that particular night. He had been left in the kitchen with a bowl of dog biscuits and some water, and in his fright he had wet the floor. Previously, as soon as the air-raid siren sounded he had gone to the front door and had stood scratching it and wagging his tail. From then on, as soon as the siren sounded, he rushed to the door and started to bark and whine until he was allowed to run down to the shelter.

★★★

Ever since I was small, I had been fascinated by railway engines. At that time they were powered by steam, and to me they seemed to be almost alive, huffing and puffing in much the same way as I did. Fortunately for Richard and me, the main line of the London, Midland and Scottish Railway – the LMS – ran within less than half a mile of our home, which together with the accompanying marshalling yards and adjacent power station were the reasons the Germans repeatedly bombed our part of Wembley. However, as there was no more bombing in our area during the remaining weeks of the spring of 1943, I began to collect train numbers, accompanied by Richard and his friend Christopher Young and my friend Lawrence, a hobby that kept us busy and out of harm's way on fine days. The site from which we watched out for trains was an iron pedestrian bridge known as the Iron Bridge, running over the railway and marshalling yards at the nearest point to our homes. For hours we stood watching and chatting on the steps of the bridge right alongside the railway track. Our reward happened every ten to fifteen minutes or so as a train pulled by a well-known steam engine raced towards us on its way to cities in the north, such as Manchester, Birmingham, Liverpool, Blackpool, Crewe and Glasgow, or in the reverse direction towards Euston, the main-line train station in London, where the trains terminated, a few miles south of where we were standing.

Each engine had a name and a number or, if they were less prestigious, only a number. Our aim was to collect as many engine names and numbers as possible and enter them into a notebook or, a year or so later, into one of the newly published ABC books of train numbers and names produced by a man named Ian Allan.

I remember standing on the bridge on one particular morning during our summer holidays. As soon as we saw our first train approaching, Christopher shouted, 'It's a mainliner!' while it was still about a mile away.

In anticipation, I became more alert and began to move and shuffle my feet on the step of the bridge on which I was standing.

When the great beast was about a quarter of a mile away, we could see it rocking from side to side in a cloud of steam as it came roaring towards us with a plume of smoke issuing from its funnel and trailing behind it.

'It's a streamliner!' Christopher shouted, referring to an engine with a streamlined front and a name such as *King George VI* or *Duchess of Hamilton*. If it wasn't a streamliner, the shout was likely to be 'It looks like a Royal Scot!' referring to a conventionally shaped engine with a name such as *Royal Scott, Royal Scots Grey, Sherwood Forester* or *Royal Fusilier*.

When the train was a couple of hundred yards away, the bridge began to shake and we could hear the engine snorting. A few seconds later it was upon us, its huge wheels and the piston driving them just 4 or 5ft from where we were standing. In a panic we looked up to see if we could catch a glimpse of the nameplate on its gleaming body. In a blur I caught sight of the words *King George VI*.

Then it had disappeared, and the carriages were thundering passed.

'Did you see that! *King George VI*!' Richard shouted above the noise.

The others agreed, as the last of the carriages slipped passed and disappeared through the bridge over the platforms at Wembley Central Station.

While we were waiting for the next train, Richard said, 'I am going to put a penny on the line and see if it gets flattened when the train goes over it.'

To place anything on the line was against the law and could be dangerous but, before I could stop him, Richard had climbed onto the handrail at the side of the bridge and, looking both ways to make sure a train wasn't approaching, had dropped onto the ground beside the track and carefully placed a penny on the rail nearest us, before climbing back.

'You'll be in terrible trouble if anything awful happens,' I warned him.

We had only to wait a few minutes.

As the train approached, I wondered if anything untoward would happen.

'It's got the long boiler of a Royal Scot!' Lawrence shouted.

He was right. It was the *Sherwood Forester*, one of the Royal Scot class.

When it had passed, we watched as Richard climbed back over the side of the bridge and retrieved the penny that was now squashed very thin.

'Don't say anything to Mum and Dad,' he said, putting the penny into his pocket.

After that one of us often climbed over the side of the bridge and placed a penny on the line.

A year or so later, we were considered old enough by Mum and Dad to go by Underground train to the nearest main-line railway stations in the centre of London, where we collected more train numbers. On one occasion, when we were at King's Cross Station we saw *Mallard*, belonging to LNER – the London and North Eastern Railway. It was the fastest engine in the world, having attained a speed of 126mph.

Sometimes, when we were at one of London's mainline stations, an engine driver would allow one or two of us the ultimate thrill of climbing up into the cab of an engine and standing on the footplate to admire the furnace, glowing red and yellow, and the dials that recorded the pressure of the steam in the boilers. When we were a little older, occasionally we would trespass onto a railway line and make our way along the edge of the track to an engine shed, where engines were being serviced and repaired. Sometimes the men working on the engines would chase us away; at other times they would allow us to walk around an engine and occasionally to climb up onto a footplate to admire the control centre of the great beast.

★★★

Apart from collecting train numbers, during the summer holidays of 1943 I became friendly with and played with two new groups of boys. One group was composed of boys living in Bassingham Road, about a quarter of a mile from the shop; the other was of boys living in Holland Road, a little further away from the shop than Bassingham Road.

The boys from Bassingham Road were a gang led by a boy named Victor, who was several years older than I was, and stood head and shoulders above me. Each time we met, he held court and discussed with us what we should do. Usually, it involved moving through the bushes of the Old Field like a herd of cattle, feeling powerful; in our minds we were seeking out other gangs we could intimidate, although fortunately for us, only very occasionally did we meet any. If we did, it was a matter of staring out one another rather than fisticuffs.

The mother of one of the boys, a blond chap named John who wore glasses, worked in a factory making arms for the war effort. Every now and again, she slipped a few of the army pocket knives she had made into her handbag and gave them to John to distribute to us. The knives were big and heavy and had black Bakelite sides, a bottle opener, a spike for getting stones out of horses' hooves, and two blades – everything a boy might imagine he wanted. And I wanted one. But there were other boys to be supplied before me, and I had to wait until one afternoon when we had gathered at the Bassingham Road entrance to the Old Field and were trying to decide what we should do. As we were talking, John reached into his trouser pocket and handed me a knife. For the next day or so I was in heaven. I had everything in the world I could possibly want, and later that afternoon, with the knife safely stashed away in my pocket, I enjoyed the way it knocked against my thigh with each step that I took.

On another occasion when I joined the gang, John whispered to me that a woman was sunbathing in the nude in the back garden of a house in nearby Holland Road. That was all I needed to know! Half the population might be female, but the only ones I ever saw were fully dressed. Now perhaps, I had a chance to see what one really looked like without any clothes.

Leaving the gang, I went to find Richard, who was playing on the swings on One Tree Hill, a park adjacent to the Old Field.

'Listen, Rich!' I said, 'Get off that swing! I've got some news for you. A woman's lying naked, sunbathing in her garden next to the Old Field.'

Richard did not need any further encouragement. 'Let's get going!' he said without hesitation.

The garden in which the naked woman was said to be lying was at the corner of a line of gardens jutting into the Old Field. It was surrounded by a high wall made of breeze blocks cemented together, and topped by a line of sharp stones. Fortunately, there was a row of bushes and trees running parallel with the wall. A tree adjacent to the garden in which the woman was said to be lying had branches sticking out from its trunk that made it ideal for climbing. Followed by Richard, I climbed the tree until I was about 5ft above the top of the wall, at which height we were completely hidden by foliage.

It didn't occur to either of us that by spying on the woman we might be invading her privacy. So far as we were concerned, what we were doing was exciting, and it was her fault if she was lying there naked.

I parted the leaves in front of me and looked. There she was! 'Wow!' I said softly to myself. 'There she blows!' referring to a story I had just been reading about a whale.

But it wasn't a whale I was looking at! It was a woman without any clothes lying on a camp bed in the middle of the lawn. Her legs were crossed and her feet were towards us. Her head was supported by her flexed right arm and in her left hand was a book she was reading. About the rest, there isn't much to say, except that her chest looked very different to mine! As for the rest … well … it was hidden by her crossed legs.

Anticlimax? Not on your nelly! I had seen a naked woman, although apart from the thrill of the forbidden, in a vague sort of way I was left wondering what all the fuss was about. A few years later, I would know full well.

# 12

# A CHANGE
# OF SCHOOLS

In the autumn of 1943 it was time for me to leave
Wembley House School and go to a school for older
boys. The three best schools in the local area of London
in which I lived were the Lower School of John Lyon
in Harrow, so called because the Upper School was the
Harrow Public School, which everyone knows about.
The other schools were Upper Latymer, founded in
1646, twenty years before the Great Fire of London; and
St Clement Danes, an upmarket grammar school. For reasons that I do not remember, Dad wanted me to go to
either John Lyon School or St Clement Danes. Getting
to John Lyon School would involve a short journey by
Underground train away from the centre of London and
deeper into suburbia; the journey to St Clement Danes
was also by Underground train but in the opposite direction, towards the centre of the city.

One morning in the autumn of 1943 Dad accompanied me to John Lyon School, where I was interviewed by the headmaster, Mr Le Beau, in his study with Dad sitting beside him. To me, aged 10, everyone aged over about 50 seemed to be old and, with his thick white hair, Mr Le Beau was no exception, although from his friendly manner, I perceived him to be a kind man. After a few general questions about the things I had learnt at Wembley House School and the games I played there, he asked me to read a page from a book he handed me. I stood in front of him with Dad looking on, wondering how I would do? I was good at maths, but was a poor reader, and was flummoxed when I came to the word chimney. I had not seen it before, and when speaking about a chimney, I said chimley.

Twenty seconds of silence ensued.

'Do you know the word you're having difficulty with?' Mr Le Beau asked.

'No, Sir. I'm sorry …'

Mr Le Beau asked me to come over to him, and show him the word I could not read.

'Ah! Chimney! That's a difficult word!' he said. 'Not to worry. For the rest of your life always keep a dictionary beside you when you are reading, and look up any word you don't understand.' He turned to Dad. 'An honest young man! He didn't try to prevaricate.'

In the weeks that followed, I took the entrance exams for the two schools that Dad wanted me to go to, and a week or so later, as I was in the kitchen laying the table for lunch, he came in smiling with several letters in his hand. He told me that I had passed the entrance exams to both schools. 'Well done!' he said. 'You can choose. Which one do you think you would like to go to?'

He towered over me. I knew which school I would like to go to, but was hesitant about saying so, as I didn't want to burden Mum and Dad with any unnecessary expenses. Throughout my life they had repeatedly told Richard and me that money was in short supply, and that we had to be careful about spending it. There were no fees at St Clement Danes. By contrast, John Lyon School charged £8 12s 6d per term, which was more than a week's pay for a skilled working man at that time, and allowing for inflation, about £395 today, although in fact, today the fees at the school are well over £6,000 per term.

'Well?' Dad asked kindly.

Hesitating, I replied, 'If you and Mum can afford it, I would like to go to John Lyon School, if that's OK?'

'That's fine! That's the one I would prefer you to go to,' Dad replied.

On my last day at Wembley House School I went round the classrooms saying goodbye to my friends and the teachers I had known for four years, and was surprised by how upset I was at the prospect of leaving. To me, the school was my second home, a place I knew and in which I felt secure, and I could barely hold back my tears. I felt as if I was being torn in two. But I didn't want to cry, as I had been bought up to believe that men – even little men like me – don't cry. But I couldn't help myself, I was so upset that when I had completed saying goodbye I made my way to the boys' toilet, where, shutting and locking the door, I leaned against the wall and howled my eyes out. 'I don't want to leave!' I sobbed. 'I don't want to leave ...'

Eventually, when everyone had left the building, I slunk away, but I didn't go home, as I was embarrassed by my red eyes, and so I walked the streets, avoiding people until I felt more composed and assumed that my eyes were no longer red.

★★★

Christmas 1943 was a bleak time. Rationing was probably at its worst. Few families were lucky enough to find a turkey. Mum got a chicken for us, but it was a tough old rooster, possibly several years old, and so tough that after trying to eat it, everyone in the family except me gave up and just ate the vegetables that Mum had cooked with it. I tried to eat it for a little longer, but in the end even I was forced to give up.

★★★

On a cold winter's morning in January 1944, a few days before my eleventh birthday, Dad took me by Underground train to South Harrow Station from where we walked up half a mile to John Lyon School. Outside he signalled goodbye.

'I'll come with you tomorrow, then if you are happy, you can do it on your own,' he said.

I was confident about making the journey on my own, as I had travelled by train with Richard and our friends to the centre of London to collect train numbers on many occasions, but Dad wanted to make sure that I was safe.

John Lyon School was very different to Wembley House School. At Wembley House School, the classrooms in which I had been taught were simply large rooms in a big old house, with a garden at its back that acted as its playground. At John Lyon School, the classroom in which I was a pupil was on the first floor of an old Victorian building. In some ways, the room resembled the inside of a church, as it had large, tall windows; walls about a foot thick; and a ceiling almost 20ft above us.

The class consisted of thirty keen boys like me. During our first morning there, Mr Le Beau came in and told each of us how we had done in the entrance exam. Apparently, I had done well in maths. Mr Le Beau then went on to tell us that the school had been founded in the nineteenth century for middle-class boys who lived within a radius of about 6 or 7 miles of the school. Merchant Taylors' and Haberdashers' served a similar function in other parts of London. St Paul's and Westminster were a bit more prestigious. The Harrow School that most people have heard of had been founded in 1572 by John Lyon to serve the local population, but over the centuries had become the exclusive boarding school that is now famous throughout the world. Harrow School and John Lyon School were linked in various ways, and shared the same motto, school badge and school song.

Later, I learnt that, in general, boys from John Lyon School went into commerce, the Civil Service and professions such as medicine and the law. A few went into the armed services via Sandhurst, Cranbourne or Dartmouth, and others into management, particularly into companies such as W.H. Wills, the tobacco company that had factories and offices at Park Royal, about 4 or 5 miles from the school. To me, even though I was only 11, nothing seemed worse than the prospect of being a manager in a large company as, somewhere inside me, I knew that I didn't want to work in an office.

The ability of the masters to control classes varied. Even though we were only young boys, our relationship with the masters was dominated by group dynamics. Almost without being aware of it, we probed each master's strengths and weaknesses. The personality of the master determined whether there was order or disorder in their class. Some masters were able to keep order without saying a word. Their presence was all that was necessary to render us docile and attentive. For others, keeping order was an almost impossible task. Sometimes, the ones who couldn't keep order were the ones we loved, while others who kept order through fear were hated.

I have very clear memories of many of the masters. The headmaster Mr Le Beau reminded me of Mr Chips from the film *Goodbye Mr Chips* that I had seen with Richard and Mum and Dad just before the war. His only interest was the school. Mr Le Beau told us that as a young man he had travelled to South Africa and several other countries. But that was long in the past. When I was at the school, he walked about in a Homburg hat, a stiff white collar attached by studs to the front and back of his shirt, and an old blue pinstriped suit, the trousers of which were too short, and revealed the high-sided, old-fashioned, lace-up, patent leather boots he wore. He was like one of the boys to whom he taught chemistry – pink skinned and chubby cheeked. Only his white hair indicated otherwise. He had his likes and dislikes among the boys. I wanted to be among those whom he liked, but I was not one of his favourites, and he left me with a feeling of being an outsider.

My form master during my first term at the school was
a man named Mr Mogg. Moggy, as we called him, taught
maths. He seemed very old to us, but must have been aged
all of 40, and if he is still alive – which I doubt – he must
be a very old man. His hair was parted neatly down the
middle and was smarmed down with Brylcreem. It was
rumoured that he wore a corset. Like most of the masters,
and indeed most men at that time, he smoked heavily and
as a result his teeth were stained brown. We were a captive
audience and, apart from teaching us maths, he took
advantage of our tender years by showing off in front of
us. Standing with his hands on his hips, he harangued us
about the shortcomings of the government and told us
how he, Mr Mogg, would cure all the nation's ills if he
were prime minister. Then, having delivered one of his
diatribes, he would pace up and down on the dais that
elevated him above us, and stop and leer at us to check
that we were not laughing at him. No doubt, he thought
he was very important, but even though I was only a
young boy, and as yet had very little psychological insight,
I knew there was something suspicious and phoney about
his posturing.

History was taught by a squat, thickset, middle-aged
Irishman with long silver hair. We loved Mr Hughes,
whom we called Spike, but he could not keep order in the
class, and we made life hell for him, poor man. Because
of the pandemonium we created during his class, I don't
think I learnt much history, although I do remember a bit
about the medieval age, and the Tudor kings and queens
and Queen Elizabeth I. When the pandemonium became
too great, Mr Hughes would look at the worst offender
and say, in his soft Irish brogue, 'Oh, my god, if I get hold

149

of you, your own mother won't know you!' But nothing ever came of his threats.

The worst offender in the class was a boy named John Bragg. So that Mr Hughes couldn't get at him, each time we had a history lesson, we constructed what we called 'the Bragg Defence System'. This involved placing Bragg in the centre of the class, and moving our desks into a solid phalanx round him. This left poor Mr Hughes running round the outside of the class, muttering, 'Oh, my god! Oh, my god! If I get hold of you ...'

On one occasion when the trouble became too great, Mr Le Beau came in. Suddenly, everyone was quiet. But although Mr Le Beau gave us a ticking off, it didn't resolve the problem.

Among the English and geography teachers was a huge man named Mr Anderson. He had no problem in keeping order. One look at his huge rugged frame and enormous hands was enough to quell even the most rebellious boy. It was rumoured that as a young man he had sailed before the mast on sailing ships in the Merchant Navy, and his raw looks certainly fitted that idea. The cheeks of his face were covered by hundreds of small veins that looked as if they might be part of a ship's chart.

I didn't like Mr Anderson, but he did me a power of good. When we were reading *Treasure Island,* he organised a competition to see who could produce the best map of the island, showing where the treasure was buried. He told me to repeat my first attempt, and whispered in my ear that if I didn't very quickly produce something that met with his approval, I would feel the weight of his huge hand upon me. It had the desired effect. That evening, on my way home, I stopped at the stationers at the bottom of Harrow Hill and bought several pieces of tracing paper that I could ill afford. Then, with some Indian ink that Dad provided, I produced a map that was sufficiently good to meet with Mr Anderson's approval, and to be exhibited in front of the class along with two others.

A few days later, Mr Anderson told me and a boy named Cox to stay behind at the end of the day. Neither of us knew what he wanted, but when it came, the message was clear and simple. Either we recognised that we had more ability than we cared to admit, and set about realising our full potential, or we would feel the full weight of his personality and hand upon us. It was a threat that could not be ignored and it had a salutatory affect upon me, which reflects how important a master can be in a boy's life. Within a few weeks I went from being an average student, who regularly came twelfth out of thirty, to consistently being fourth or fifth, and often higher, in the class.

Many years later I met a schoolmaster on a train, who told me with a twinkle in his eye that it doesn't matter how much you encourage a boy, so long as it is low enough and hard enough. He was joking, of course, but my experience with Mr Anderson suggests that we all perform better when we are stimulated by a little fear and that, delivered at the right time, the threat of unpleasant consequences can concentrate the mind and is probably not a bad idea.

Latin was taught by a man whose development seemed to have been arrested when he was aged about 20. Mr Calder was like a sour overgrown schoolboy, who had never lived in the world outside school and university. His face was ravaged by years of heavy smoking, and by the time I knew him he looked like a walking cadaver with piercing blue eyes shining out of a skull-like face. In contrast to his face, his hair was thick and cut short back and sides, and was still brown and young-looking. Like Mr Anderson, he had no difficulty in keeping order. Leering at us with his piercing blue eyes, and talking in a precise, clipped Oxford accent, he kept order by using destructive sarcasm, as a consequence of which he was known as Sarky. Most of his abuse was heaped upon a poor chap named Fieldhouse.

'And there in the slime of the swamp,' he would say from the dais on which he was seated, as he fixed his gaze upon the hapless Fieldhouse, 'you will see the pink face of Fieldhouse grinning aimlessly up at you from the slime. Fieldhouse, you are so twisted that you could stand up a spiral staircase without twisting!'

Poor Fieldhouse! He bore the insults with great fortitude. But he wasn't the only one to attract Mr Calder's attention. One day, when Mr Calder was talking to us about the vanguard of the Roman army, he noticed that I wasn't paying attention and picked on me.

'Model!' he said, 'How many wheels were there on the van of the Roman army?'

Startled at the sound of my name, I looked about helplessly, wondering how to answer. I had no idea what he was talking about, but a friend of mine named Gerald, who was sitting in a desk behind me, whispered, 'Four! Tell him there were four wheels on the van of the Roman army.'

Thinking I was out of trouble, I repeated what Gerald had told me.

'Four, sir,' I said. 'The van of the Roman army had four wheels.'

The class broke into laughter, and even Mr Calder couldn't help smiling. 'You horrible fool!' he said. 'Don't ever let me catch you again not paying attention!'

He then christened me 'Henry', after a fictional schoolboy character from the literature of the earlier part of the century, and for the rest of my days at John Lyon School that was the name by which I was known.

Physics and some maths were taught by a squat, dark Welshman who looked as if he had just come out of a coal mine. Taffy Williams was such a good teacher that, much to my surprise, following Mr Anderson's encouragement, I came first in his class. I saw through Taffy's slightly bellicose manner to the gentle person inside, and all these years later still remember him with affection. He was like a pit pony. Earlier in his life, he had invented the word 'Bodmas' that featured in many maths textbooks of that time, as it indicated the order in which mathematical calculations should be made, namely – *B*rackets before *O*ver, before *D*ivision, before *M*ultiplication, before *A*ddition, before *S*ubtraction. He was also a bit of a showman. One of his tricks was to write on the blackboard with both hands simultaneously, his right hand writing forwards and his left hand writing backwards.

One day, after he had explained Boyle's law to us, a friend of mine named Bob Meadowmead asked him, 'How d'you know that, then, sir?' to which Taffy replied angrily in his lilting Welsh voice, 'I know, that's how I know! I'll come down there and knock half your bloody block off!'

Apart from Mr Mogg, maths was also taught by Lt Colonel Wilson – or Willie as we called him. We loved Willie. There was something slightly buccaneer and irreverent about him that we related to. During the First World War he had been a lieutenant colonel in the army, and he had the pink scrubbed face of an old soldier. He was so closely shaved that it looked as if he had scraped a layer of skin from his face. He liked us to joke around a little with him, but didn't have any difficulty keeping order. Instinctively, we knew just how far we could go with him, and that if we went beyond the unspoken boundaries he allowed us, he would say, 'Get out! I hate you and I hate your mother, and I hate your father for having you! Go and stand outside in the corridor for fifteen minutes!'

Embarrassed, whoever it was who had offended him would get up from his desk and silently slink out of the class. Then, at the end of the prescribed time, with a wink at the rest of us, Willie would say, 'Go out and fetch him in! He's done his time. Bring him back in!' In response, one of the boys in the front row of the class would get up and bring the offender in, who, with an embarrassed grin on his face, would sit down at his desk as inconspicuously as possible.

When he was angry, Willie would say, 'If you're not careful I'll come down there and poke my finger in your eye!'

It sounds dreadful, but to us it was part of the fun, and we would all laugh.

Willie had his favourites, and fortunately I was one of them. Generally, he liked spirited boys who would respond to his repartee, but he could be unpredictable. On one of my reports he wrote, 'This boy could be at the top of the class if he wasn't so prone to fooling around.'

I was standing in Mum and Dad's bedroom by Dad's side of their bed, waiting as Dad read the report, fully expecting it to be very good, and I was surprised by

Willie's comment, but not as surprised as Dad. 'What do you mean by fooling around when I pay so much money for you to go to that school?' he demanded angrily.

I was dumbstruck. As Willie encouraged us to fool around, and as I had come fifth in maths, which was near the top of the class, I could not understand how he could have written such a thing, but I was too speechless to say anything to Dad in my defence.

In addition to maths, Willie ran the school choir and the OTC – the Officers' Training Corps – which during my time at the school had its name changed to the more democratic Army Cadet Force. At morning prayers in the assembly hall, Willie would beam with pleasure as the whole school sang such favourite hymns as 'Onward Christian Soldiers', 'All Things Bright and Beautiful' and 'Rock of Ages'. On the odd occasions that we did not sing well, he would glower and, later in the day, would ask each class he taught why they hadn't sung well that morning.

In the higher forms, geography was taught by Major Sibcy, or Basher as we called him, although why he was called that I do not know as corporal punishment was uncommon at John Lyon School. Basher didn't have to keep order. One look at us, and we knew he would not stand any nonsense. If a boy started to play up, he would look up at him and say in a tired voice, 'Jones! [Or whatever the boy's name was] Stop being tiresome,' and Jones would immediately stop being tiresome.

French was taught from the fourth form upwards by a terrible man named Dr Hurst, whom we feared and loathed from the first day that we met him. We were sitting quietly at our desks, chatting among ourselves, as we waited for him to appear on his first morning at the school. Suddenly, the door of the classroom smashed shut with such a loud bang that we all swung round to see what had happened.

Standing in the entrance to the room with his feet planted firmly apart was a formidable-looking middle-aged man who appeared to be more like the commandant of a prison camp than a schoolmaster. He was wearing a dark blue suit, his hair was oiled and combed straight back without a parting, and his mouth had a cruel, turned-down shape, like the mouth of a fish.

'My name is Dr Hurst, and I will not tolerate any disorder!' he shouted at us in a drill sergeant's voice. 'Sit down, and be quiet!'

He stared at us with penetrating dark, almost black, eyes and told us that he had been an officer in the Dragoon Guards, and that he expected us to be as quiet and as disciplined as a company of soldiers. Suitably cowed, we listened quietly as he told us how he would achieve his aim of making us fluent in French by giving us large tracts of the language to learn by heart, and by keeping us in after school if we could not repeat them in a word-perfect fashion.

But although he was hateful, and I didn't like the way he ruled us by fear, I have to admit that there must have been a streak of kindness in him somewhere. In the fifth form, I panicked when I was called in to take the oral exam in French for the School Certificate – the equivalent of today's GCSEs – and apart from saying 'Bonjour, Monsieur,' as I entered the room, I was unable to utter a word to the external examiner, who had come all the way from London University to examine us.

My mind was frozen with fear, and all I could see as I struggled helplessly to understand what the examiner was saying were his metal-rimmed half spectacles and small goatee beard. Everything else in my mind was obliterated, and I was even unable to enunciate a word of English, let alone French. After a few seconds, the examiner switched topics and asked me another question in French, but I was hardly able to hear him, let alone reply. Sensing my predicament after perhaps half a minute of silence, during which I waited miserably to be dismissed, Dr Hurst, who was sitting beside the external examiner, gave a throaty cough and, leaning towards the examiner, said very quietly, 'This one is very shy. I think we'd better let him go.'

With that I was allowed to leave the room. But Dr Hurst must have said something to the examiner in my favour, or else I must have done very well in the written part of the exam, as I didn't just get a bare Pass, but was awarded a Credit in French. Many years later, along with the four Credits and a Distinction I obtained in other subjects, I was able to use that Credit in French to prove that I had matriculated, and as a result was able to go to university without any A levels, which by then were the generally required entry qualifications.

***

Some of my happiest days during my later years at John Lyon School were caddying at weekends and during holidays for Dad, when he played golf. For a day's caddying, he paid me 10s, or 50p in today's money.

For some years, his handicap was three, but gradually it increased to twelve as he became older. Over the years I got to know enough about the game to be able to advise him when I thought the head of his club wasn't quite in line with the direction in which he wished the ball to travel. At one time I even toyed with the idea of becoming a golf professional, although as it turned out, it would not have been compatible with the career I did choose.

Dad was a member of Sudbury Golf Club, although he also loved playing at the golf clubs at Sunningdale, Wentworth and the High Course at Moor Park. Nothing gave him greater pleasure than being on a golf course on a dry, overcast autumn day, when the trees were still heavy and green and the leaves had not yet turned yellow. England then was in all her glory, and for me as I trailed along behind him, with his golf bag hanging from my shoulder, the problems of growing up seemed far away.

Among the men with whom he played was a dried-up, retired professor of English from Oxford, the floor manager of the famous 400 Night Club in Leicester Square in the centre of London, and the retired headmaster of a Jewish boarding school for boys. Gibby the floor manager was my favourite. When a game lasted too long, and Dad was likely to get into trouble from Mum for being late home for lunch, Gibby would buy a bouquet of flowers, accompany us home and present it to Mum as a peace offering.

# 13

# A MILKLADY AND
# A FARAWAY BATTLE

One day during the early part of the Easter holidays in the spring of 1944, after I had been at John Lyon School for three months, I saw an Express Dairies milk float being drawn by a horse in a street about a quarter of a mile behind my home. Before the war the round would have been done by a man, but because so many men were away, it was being done a woman. I watched the milklady deliver milk to one or two houses, then plucking up courage, I walked over to her and asked if she would allow me to help her.

'You can if you like,' she said indifferently. 'But I'm in a hurry. I'm very busy. I won't be able to pay you, you know.'

I did not want money. I wanted to ride the float and be with the horse, which was black and eating oats from a nosebag while it waited to be told to move on.

The milklady's name was Anne. Her hair was dark and wiry, and her face was prematurely lined from years of smoking. She gave me a couple of bottles of milk, and told me to place them on the side of the doorstep of No. 14, a small terraced house on the left-hand side of the road.

When I came back, I patted the horse and walked beside it as it moved a couple of houses along the street. When it stopped, Anne gave me a bottle of milk, and asked me to take it to No. 18.

In a quarter of an hour we had finished the round in that street and had moved onto the next street, and for the rest of the morning I helped Anne deliver milk to all the houses on her round. Occasionally, we stopped so she could roll and smoke a cigarette.

'Can I come tomorrow?' I asked, as she prepared to move off to the dairy's depot.

'If you wish,' she replied. 'You were very helpful. With your help, I've finished early today.'

I joined her every day of that week and the following week, and each day rode in the front of the float when she did.

At the end of the two weeks, she gave me half a crown, 12½p in today's money, and allowed me to take the reins of the horse on the way back to the depot, where I helped her to take him from the shafts of the float, place him in his stall, lather him down and give him a meal of oats.

★★★

While I was helping Anne, faraway on the far side of the world, at a little settlement in the hills separating India from Burma, my cousin Gordon, Aunty Rose's middle son, was taking part in an unsung major battle that has been almost forgotten. The Battle of Kohima was fought from 3 April to 22 April 1944 and was one of the most bitterly contested battles of the Second World War, having been likened in importance to the much better-known, larger Battle of El-Alamein in North Africa. Much of the battle at Kohima was fought at close quarters, with the opposing armies separated by only a few yards.

Like his brother Maurice, Gordon had volunteered for the army at the beginning of the war, and subsequently had risen to the rank of captain before being seconded to the Indian Army. He was unwell for years after he returned from India, and he rarely spoke about the battle. But, just before he died, he told me about it while we were having lunch with our wives at Lemonia, a well-known Greek restaurant near Primrose Hill, a little to the north of central London.

Kohima was (and still is) a small hilltop settlement on a pass separating India from Burma (now Myanmar). To get from Burma into India, the Japanese would have to destroy the British and Indian forces based in Kohima and nearby Imphal.

At Kohima, the Japanese had 15,000 soldiers and were confident of advancing into India. Opposing them, the British and Indian forces amounted to just 2,500 men. Until that time in the war, as they advanced through South East Asia, the Japanese had met with only relatively light resistance from the British. At Singapore, 80,000 British, Commonwealth and Empire troops had ignominiously surrendered to the Japanese on one of the darkest days in the military history of the British Empire. At Kohima and Imphal the Japanese learnt that, despite the terrible odds against the Allied soldiers and the multiple casualties they suffered, British and Indian soldiers were not only able to match them, but to outfight them.

Gordon told me that, for day upon terrible day, the Japanese threw wave upon wave of men at the British and Indian lines, and that at one time only the width of the settlement's tennis court separated them. Piles of Japanese bodies mouldered and decayed in front of the Allied lines.

On 22 April, the exhausted Japanese began to retreat back into Burma, many of them dying on the way from starvation and tropical diseases.

The battle was a great victory for the British and Indian forces, and after the war a memorial was erected at Kohima bearing the words:

When you go home
Tell them of us, and say:
For your tomorrow,
We gave our today.

# 14

# SCHOOL MATTERS

My best friend at John Lyon School was Gerald Godfrey, the boy who had told me to say that the van of the Roman army had four wheels when I was asked about it by Mr Calder. Gerald was clever and good at languages, and was said by his father to sit for hours reading the *Encyclopædia Britannica*. He was also a bit of a clown and a showman and was popular with the other boys in our class, although he irritated some of the masters.

In contrast with him, I was still very shy and hopeless about anything that required a hint of acting. For fear of drawing attention to myself, I strove to avoid reading aloud in class or singing in the school choir, as the latter involved being auditioned. If a master looked around the class for someone to read aloud, I would crouch behind the boy in front of me and hope that I would not be seen. If I was unlucky enough to be spotted and be asked to read, I would suffer agonies of embarrassment and would hardly be able to see the words on the page.

But things gradually changed, and as the years passed, I became more confident and more aware of myself and the world around me. I was growing up and was becoming an independent-minded young man. By then, Richard and I were good friends and no longer fought. He had joined me at John Lyon School, and as his older brother I tended to watch over and protect him. When he was in the second form, and I was 15 and in the fifth form, I had a splendid fight on his behalf with a prefect named Miller. Miller had accused Richard of some minor misdemeanour and had beaten him up and made him cry for denying that he had committed it.

Miller was in the prefect's room when I found him. Several other prefects were in the room with him, but I did not hesitate to go for him. 'I'll teach you to beat up my younger brother for nothing!' I shouted at him. I jumped on him and started to pummel him with my fists for all I was worth. We tumbled to the floor and I fell on top of him, continuing the punches. After about half a minute, I was dragged off him and punched by several of the prefects, who had been watching.

A few minutes later, I was arraigned before a hastily convened committee of prefects and was harangued in no uncertain terms by the school's head boy. 'Model!' he said, 'You're the sort of boy we don't want at this school.' As he was bumptious and behaved as if he had a hotline to God, I didn't take much notice of him or his swanky upper-crust accent. So OK, I had taken a good hiding. But so what! I had given Miller a bloody nose, and afterwards he was wary of me and respected me.

Later that term, I ran round the corner of a building at the school and collided with a tall lanky boy named

Plummer. Our heads smashed into one another and we each suffered a deep laceration just below the eyebrow of one of our eyes. Plummer was concussed and had to go home, and was away from school for several days. I went back to my classroom with a plaster over my eye. Later that afternoon, a message was delivered to the class, informing me that Mr Le Beau wanted to see me in his study. I was apprehensive, as I hurried across the playground to the Old Building in which his study was situated. Perhaps he was going to blame me and tell me off for hurting Plummer. But I was wrong. To my surprise, Mr Le Beau gave me a couple of chocolates from a box he kept for special occasions.

'How are you, then, Model, boy?' he asked, smiling broadly and leaning towards me from the chair in which he was sitting. 'I hear it was quite a collision. Are you sure you are able to go on with your class? If you want, you can go home.'

When I said that I preferred to stay, he smiled and said. 'Good man; you're a tough one.'

I felt privileged and that colliding with Plummer was almost worthwhile, and I savoured the feeling for the rest of that day.

\*\*\*

Earlier, I described the idiosyncrasies of some of the masters at John Lyon School, but there is no doubt that the academic education I received there was very good, particularly if you were in the 'A' stream of your year, as I was lucky enough to be. But there was an adverse aspect of the education there. Although I wasn't conscious of it at the time, imperceptibly, from my first day at the school, I was gradually drawn away from the social fabric I knew in Wembley and instead was inculcated with a new ethos – the ethos of the public school and its middle-class values. Many of those values were a reflection of the snobbishness that permeated British society in the 1930s and '40s. Instead of appreciating their good fortune at being relatively well off, at that time many middle-class people used their relative wealth and the way of life it afforded them, to distance themselves from and elevate themselves above the mass of the people, who were expected to 'know their place' and sadly often did. Within broad limits, middle-class people judged others by their job, the school they had been to, the way they spoke and such trivial matters as the way they held their knife and fork, rather than by the sort of person they were. Despite ability, doors were closed to people whose manners and background were considered to be 'not quite right'.

At Wembley House School, the teachers had been women who wore everyday clothes. At John Lyon School, the teachers were all men who wore black academic gowns over their suits and carried or wore mortarboards. They made no secret of their feelings about their elevated position, as they saw it, in society.

No longer was I free to roam all over north-west London on Saturdays with Richard and the girls, Betty and Margaret, from next door. Instead, I had to attend school on Saturday mornings and, depending upon the season of the year, I had to play either football or cricket on Wednesday and Saturday afternoons.

At school, I found myself unconsciously drawn to and making friends with boys from backgrounds that I judged were not very dissimilar to my own, and whose parents no doubt wanted their sons to enjoy a better chance in life than they had enjoyed.

Fortunately, the changes imposed upon me did not affect my feelings towards Mum and Dad, who I have to say, were impervious to such things and were a healthy counterbalance to them. Mum in particular was an example, mixing – if she wished – with anyone who was decent, no matter what their background, race or religion. Even so, I began to feel distant from the shopkeepers I knew so well in the parade of shops in which we lived. In a word, without being conscious of it, I was being moulded into a person who was different to the person I had been, although it was so slow and subtle that it would be many years before I would realise what had happened. Some might say that I was simply growing up. But I don't think it was that simple.

# 15

# GREAT EVENTS
# AND A NEW KIND
# OF BOMBING

By the early months of 1944 the south of England had become a vast armed camp as more and more troops poured in from all over the world in preparation for the invasion of France and the liberation of Europe from Nazi tyranny. There were Americans in beautiful uniforms that to me looked like expensively tailored suits; Australians in hats with broad brims turned up at the side; New Zealanders in conical hats with broad circular brims; Canadians in forage caps; officers of the Free Polish Army in shining asymmetrical hats with four sloping sides; officers of the Free French Army in smart kepis; and, of course, Indians in turbans.

Each morning, as I walked to Alperton Station and, a few minutes later, from South Harrow Station on my way to John Lyon School, I saw fleets of American Flying Fortresses like cigars with wings high up in the sky on their way to bomb Germany. As preparations for the coming invasion of Europe gathered pace, vast amounts of military equipment were assembled and stored along the sides of many main roads in rural parts of southern England. On one occasion, I saw mile upon mile of tanks; guns; snub-nosed camouflaged army lorries; and large, portable, military cooking stoves on wheels, all lying silently by the sides of the road, as the trees blossomed and the weather grew warm.

On 6 June 1944, I came down to breakfast to learn that earlier that morning Allied troops had landed on several beaches in Normandy in the greatest invasion by sea that

Armoured vehicles, guns and everyday life in southern England. (Evening Standard/Stringer/Getty Images)

the world has known. Apart from the troops, a complete harbour named Mulberry was in the process of being floated across the English Channel or La Manche (the Sleeve) as the French call it. As I ate my cornflakes at the kitchen table in the comfort of my home, I kept thinking of the young men who were fighting and dying on the French coast, not very far from where I was sitting. I kept praying, 'Please, dear God, please, let them be safe.'

Over the next few days several hundred thousand Allied soldiers were landed and fought their way towards Paris. In Britain, the atmosphere was tense as people wondered if the invasion would be successful. If not, the war might go on for years, and hundreds of thousands more people might be killed. Fortunately, the Germans had been caught unawares and were not expecting an invasion at the time it occurred or in that particular part of France, and their commander Field Marshal Erwin Rommel was at home on leave in Germany. The British and Canadians were relatively lucky, and during the land-ings suffered fairly light casualties, but for the Americans it was a different story. At Omaha Beach, the Germans were entrenched in forts on top of cliffs and were able to shoot, kill and wound thousands of American service-men as they streamed ashore. For hours it seemed that the invasion might fail and have to be called off. Only the bravery and sacrifice of the young American soldiers saved the situation.

On D-Day+1, my cousin Maurice landed in Normandy and was immediately precipitated into the fighting. The speed at which it happened reflects the way life can change so suddenly. A few hours before, he had been in a safe part of southern England; now he was suddenly in the midst of a terrible battle and facing the very real possibility of being killed. His bravery that day became part of family lore. I knew him as a dashing, somewhat distant young officer in the army, who wore a leather Sam Brown belt over his khaki dress uniform. He was married to a lady named Ruth, who throughout war was a sergeant in the WAAF – the Women's Auxiliary Air Force. I hardly knew Maurice before the war as he lived with his parents in Laindon, some 40 miles from where I lived with Mum and Dad and Richard. But I was aware that before the war he had qualified as a chartered accountant, and that, along with his brother Gordon, he had volunteered for the army soon after war was declared and subsequently had risen to the rank of major.

Later, I learnt that in Normandy he was in command of a company of troops, and that during the fighting some of them became cut off and at risk of being killed or captured. Maurice decided to rescue them. As he made his way towards them, a German soldier stood up in front of him and aimed his rifle at Maurice. Maurice lifted his right arm and, holding it extended in front of his face, took aim with his revolver and fired at the German at the very same moment that the German fired at him. The German fell down dead, but the bullet from his rifle tore into the hand of Maurice's extended arm. But for his hand, the bullet would have ripped into his face. Despite his wound, Maurice continued to move forward, and eventually rescued the men and led them to safety through land that was thought possibly to be mined. For his bravery he was awarded the Military Cross.

★★★

One evening a week or so after D–Day, Dad and I went out onto the landing outside our front door above the back of the shop to admire the sunset and watch the long summer's day slip slowly beneath the horizon. As the day faded, the silhouettes of the houses in front of us became darker and darker until they were almost black. Suddenly, an aircraft with flames trailing behind it streaked low across the almost-dark sky to our left.

'See that! Looks as if the poor fellow's on fire!' Dad said. 'I hope he parachutes out and survives.'

A moment or so later the flames disappeared, and after about half a minute we heard the boom of a distant explosion.

Two days later we learnt that we had been among the first to see a new German weapon – a rocket-propelled, pilotless aeroplane loaded with high explosive, variously known as a V1 flying bomb, buzz bomb or doodlebug. The fuel it carried was carefully calculated to run out when it was over London. When that happened, its engine stopped, the flames at its back went out and, a few seconds or a minute or so later, it crashed to earth with a tremendous explosion. So long as you could hear the engine, you knew you were safe, but as soon as the engine stopped, you knew it was about to crash and that it might crash on you.

It was a weapon designed to terrorise the ordinary population, and everyone listened with fear and a racing heart when they heard one. Where was it going to drop? Would it drop on them or their loved ones?

During the following week, a number of them exploded in London each day. Each time one was sighted, the air-raid siren was sounded. As a result, lessons at John Lyon School were interrupted throughout the day. When the

An artist recreation of a V1 flying bomb. (Keith Tarrier/Shutterstock)

siren sounded, we were told to hurry down to the school's air-raid shelters beside the cycle sheds, where we sat huddled on rows of benches, listening and chatting in low tones until the all clear sounded.

After a week of it, Mr Le Beau announced at morning prayers that because we were losing so much teaching time, we would no longer automatically be allowed down to the shelters when the siren sounded. Instead, a bugler from the school's cadet band was to be placed on the roof to keep a lookout and warn us with his bugle if he sighted a V1, in which case we were to hurry down to the shelters.

For several days the arrangement worked well, and very little teaching time was lost. But that changed about eleven o'clock one morning. I was in an art class being taught by a tall, white-haired, aristocratic-looking elderly man named Mr Phillips, who had come out of retirement to replace a young teacher named Mr Shelley, who had left the school to join the RAF. As was usual in Mr Phillips's class, we were mucking about and, when he wasn't look-ing, were throwing paper darts at one another. Suddenly, as I was attempting to draw the head of a horse, the bugle sounded at the same time as the very loud roar of an aero-plane engine was heard almost directly overhead. Without warning, a V1 had appeared over the brow of the hill on which the school was situated and had not been seen by the bugler until it was practically upon us. It was so close that the bugler felt the need to duck down behind the low brick wall in front of him. The roar of the plane's engine was so loud that my head felt as if it would burst. My heart was beating incredibly fast, and was like a Jack-in-the-box in my throat. A second or so later, the plane's engine stopped, to be followed by the most eerie silence and sense of expectancy I have ever experienced. It was as if I were in a large vacuum where time did not exist.

'Boys! Boys!' Mr Phillips shouted. 'Quick! Get under your desks!'

It was too late to run to the shelters. In an instant, my world reduced to just me. Terrified beyond description, afraid to the point of being unable to think, with my mind filled with terror and my heart beating so forcefully that it seemed that it might jump out of my mouth, I dropped to the floor and crouched under my desk with my head between my knees, waiting for the bomb to explode and blow me and my friends to smithereens. *Please dear God, I don't want to die. I don't want to die*, was all I could think.

At the next moment there was a huge explosion fol-lowed by the tinkling of glass falling around us. Crouched underneath my desk, I muttered a final plea to my maker, 'Dear God, have mercy on me … Please, please have mercy upon me … I don't want to die.'

An eerie silence followed the explosion, during which I expected the building to collapse on us. But it did not collapse, and I realised that perhaps I was going to live, and that the boys on either side of me were alive, and perhaps were going to live.

I crawled out from under my desk, and in the next moment, along with the rest of the boys in the class, I was standing up, taking stock and looking around to see what damage had been done to the building. I was alive! I had survived! I had not even been hurt! We were all alive! We had all survived! We were all going to live!

Although we were still too stunned to say much, the sense of relief among us was almost palpable. The building had not collapsed, the roof had not come down upon us, but most of the windows had been blown out and showers of glass had landed on us.

As the realisation sank in that we were safe, our minds began to function again, and we started to chatter nervously to the boys nearest to us.

Aware of the world around me again, I said to John Goodall, 'Phew! That was terrible! That was a close one!'

'Old Le Beau will have to think again!' he laughed.

'I don't mind if I do!' exclaimed my friend John Barlow, who later that year transferred to Manchester Grammar School. He was mimicking Colonel Chinstrap from the weekly radio show *ITMA* that helped keep up the nation's morale.

Very carefully, we picked glass off one another. Then, with glass crunching under our feet, we began to move about the classroom, shouting and laughing with relief.

A senior boy, a prefect, came into the class and talked to Mr Phillips for a moment.

'Boys!' Mr Phillips shouted. 'You've been splendid! Mr Le Beau wants to see you all in the main hall of the New Building. Please file out in an orderly fashion.'

Mr Le Beau was contrite. 'We will say a brief prayer for our delivery. Then you can go home for two days while the school is cleaned up,' he said. 'There probably won't be any glass in the windows for a while when you return.'

The bomb had glided 300 or 400 yards beyond the school's playground, and had hit a row of houses at the bottom of the hill, destroying three and killing two or three people.

Only one boy in my class had been hurt. It was said that a tiny fragment of glass had entered his back, and that as a result of the shock he had sustained, he developed TB. He was away for several terms but did eventually return. For the rest of us, the two days off school that Mr Le Beau had announced were a happy ending. Afterwards, there was never any question about going down to the shelters. As soon as the air-raid siren sounded, we got up from our desks and, in an orderly fashion, chatting quietly among ourselves, filed down the stairs to the shelters.

A few weeks later, the V1s were joined by V2 rockets. These were a very early form of the rockets that are now associated with the exploration of space. After flying through the stratosphere from occupied Europe, they dropped on many parts of London. Each carried a ton of high explosive, and every now and again throughout the day there were distant thuds and explosions. There was no warning, and you did not know when one might explode on you. They were simply a weapon of mass destruction and terror, designed to kill and maim innocent people.

An artist recreation of a V2 rocket launching into the sky. (RikoBest/ Shutterstock)

After a week or two of it, Dad decided that it was too dangerous for us to stay in London any longer, and so we made plans to spend a few weeks in the country. Mrs Noabes, the old lady in Buckingham with whom we had stayed at the height of the Blitz, was now too old to accommodate us. All Dad could find was a reasonably large room without any furniture in a small semi-detached house in Chalfont, a village in the Chiltern Hills about 20 miles north-west of London. The owner of the house was a woman named Mrs Baxter, whose husband was away at war. On Dad's first day off duty after renting the room, he took a bag of tools with him, and within a few hours had bought a pile of wood with which he constructed two very strong bunks for Richard and me to sleep one above the other. Mum slept on a camp bed and Dad slept on an inflatable air bed on the floor when he was off duty. Garden chairs sufficed as seats and an old primus camping stove, placed on the floor, sufficed as a cooking facility. Richard and I spent just over a month there, and attended a local school on the outskirts of Amersham, a short bus ride away. Mum joined us from Wembley each night along with Bingo, and Dad whenever he was off duty.

The village school was what was known in those days as a secondary modern school. When the headmaster learnt that I was from John Lyon School, he was so impressed that he put me in the top form with boys and girls aged 13 and 14, despite the fact that I was aged only 11. But I got on alright, and became friends with two of the toughest boys in the class. During breaks from lessons, the three of us squatted in a line of bushes against one of the fences on the periphery of the school, and I listened while they smoked and told me how much they hated school and longed to join the navy. One of them hated the headmaster and tried to make trouble in class. The headmaster tolerated the trouble for a couple of minutes, then invariably ordered the boy out of the class. When, on one occasion, he refused to go, the headmaster came down from the dais on which he was standing and tried to grab the boy by his collar and drag him out of the class. The two of them then began to fight. Eventually, they fell onto the floor between the desks, stirring up the dust. Despite the boy's size, the headmaster won, and he dragged the boy from the class and shut the door behind him.

Both the boys I was friendly with used language of a type I had not heard before. Every other word was 'f**k', and after one of them said the word 'c***' I innocently asked Mum that evening what it meant. 'That's a very bad word, dear. Don't ever let me hear you say that again,' she answered, not unkindly.

Although I was by far the youngest boy in the class, the lessons were well within my grasp. The only lesson I had difficulty with was the weekly music lesson, during which the class read music from music sheets, and sang like little angels. It was the lesson they were best at. By contrast, they had difficulty with maths and English, and quickly became bored and ceased to pay attention, and quietly played around or looked out of the window. The headmaster was surprised that I hadn't been taught to read music at John Lyon School. 'What, a school like that doesn't teach you to read music?' he asked quizzically. But the fact was that at John Lyon School the music master was away at the war, and when he came back after hostilities ceased, studying music and learning to play a musical instrument was an optional after-school activity for which parents had to pay extra.

# 16

# A COUNTRY LIFE

Richard and I made good use of our free time from school while we were in Chalfont. Almost opposite the house in which we were staying was a large house set well back behind a high privet hedge. It had a half-circle drive running up to it that opened onto the road at each end. Before the war the ends of the drive had been guarded by iron gates but, in keeping with government policy, they had been melted down as part of the war effort and been made into military vehicles.

Clearly, the house belonged to someone who was wealthy. Its front garden was grassed over, and in its centre was a large cherry tree. So you won't be surprised to learn that we were interested in the cherries that were growing on the tree. They hung like fat yellow decorations on a Christmas tree. Most had luscious red cheeks.

No boy could resist such a temptation. For several days we watched the house, and eventually decided that no one seemed to be living in it. One afternoon after school, hunched up like cats stalking prey, we stole very carefully over the grass to the tree and, reaching up, picked as many cherries as our pockets would hold. When they were full, we made our way out onto the road, and with a sigh of relief, headed towards a footpath leading through Stokes Farm. When we were at a safe distance from the farm buildings, we sat on the grass and ate our ill-gotten gains, taking care to take the cherry stones with us when we made our way back to the house in which we were staying.

When Mum and Bingo arrived later that evening, Mum asked, 'Did you have a good day at school, and what did you do afterwards?'

With Bingo jumping up to welcome us, we said that our day at school had been OK, and that afterwards we had gone for a walk along the footpath leading from Stokes Farm.

'That was nice,' Mum said.

Over the coming days, we scrumped more cherries from the big house without being caught.

A bit further along the road from Stokes Farm, a footpath led between high fences to a golf course. Behind the fences were large houses with very big gardens. Mrs Baxter told us that the garden on the left-hand side of the path had deep pits in it that, for the duration of the war, were being used by Bertram Mills circus to house wild animals during the circus's off season. We believed her, and every time we walked along the path, we thought we could hear lions and leopards roaring close by, although in retrospect, I doubt whether Mrs Baxter had told us the truth.

One Saturday afternoon when we were out for a country walk, we came to a low bridge over a fast-flowing stream. We stopped and looked over the railings of the bridge to see whether we could see any fish. In a clear pool leading upstream from the bridge we saw several brown trout, each about 10 or so inches long, waving their tails against the fast-flowing water as they strove to stay stationary without being pushed back. Again, it was a temptation no city boy could resist.

Fortunately, lying close to the bridge on one bank of the stream, was some builder's rubble in which there were discarded bricks and an old iron bar.

I don't remember who suggested what we should do, but the conversation went as follows:

'Let's make a dam with the bricks and see if we can catch any fish that try to swim over the top of it.'

'OK, but let's make a gap in the middle of the dam, and see whether, using the iron bar, we can hit any that try to swim through the gap.'

The distance between the steel girders on the underside of the bridge and the surface of the stream was about 4ft, enough for us to crouch and work without being seen. The stream was turbulent and fast flowing, and about 15ft wide and 6in deep. Richard stood on the bank and handed bricks to me, and I laid them in a straight line in the water under the bridge, leaving a gap of about a foot wide in the middle. A second line of bricks on top of the first completed the job.

With a firm grip on the iron bar, we took it in turns to wait on the downstream side of the gap and hit at any fish that tried to swim through it. At first, we were unsuccessful, but after a few swipes, one of us hit a fish and the other grabbed it from the water and placed it in the bottom of a large tin that we had found among the builder's rubble and partially filled with water. The next fish we swiped at was beheaded but edible, and was placed in the tin.

Soon we had six or seven fish. A couple had had their heads knocked off, one appeared to be unharmed and able to swim, and the others were dead.

We tipped the one that was able to swim back into the stream, emptied the water from the tin, put on our socks and shoes, carried the tin with the fish in it back to the house in which we were staying and waited for Mum and Bingo to come from London for the night.

Mum wasn't cross with us. 'I'm not sure that you should have done what you did,' she said. 'But they look good. I'll fry them and we'll have them for dinner. I'd like to give one to Bingo, but I think it'd be too bony.'

Mum fried the fish and we shared them between us with some bread, which made a very tasty meal.

A few days later, as we were walking past the parade of shops near Chalfont and Latimer Station, we fell into conversation with a young woman who was holding the reins of a white horse that was eating grass from a patch of grass by the pavement.

'You can pat him if you like,' the young woman said.

We patted the horse, as we had been bid. When she heard that we were temporary evacuees from London, the young woman laughed and asked where we were from, and when we told her, she said, 'If you meet me here tomorrow at two in the afternoon, you can ride Gee-Gee with me walking beside you.'

She told us that her name was Julie, and that she was 18 years old. She struck both of us as very beautiful.

The following afternoon she was waiting for us when we got to the parade of shops at two o'clock. We were a bit shy with one another at first, but any awkwardness soon disappeared and after we had walked a little way down a lane, away from the shops, Richard and I took turns in riding Gee-Gee, as the horse was named.

It was strange sitting on a horse for the first time, some 5 or so feet above the ground, with my legs splayed round either side of Gee-Gee's body, and even stranger when he put his head down to eat grass when we stopped. Then, it seemed as if I were sitting up high, with my legs splayed, and nothing in front of me.

Thereafter, we met Julie and rode Gee-Gee each Saturday and Sunday afternoon for the remaining two weeks that we were in Chalfont.

Towards the end of our stay in Chalfont, we found the front door of the house we were staying in locked when we got back from school. That was unusual, as the door was normally left unlocked all day, burglary in that part of the country being very uncommon during those years. After trying the door a couple times, we walked round to the back of the house and tried the back door. That too was locked. Even more puzzled, we peered through the large sash window next to the back door to see if anyone was in the small morning room next to the kitchen. Immediately below the window, we saw Mrs Baxter lying on the sofa in the embrace of a man, whom we realised instantly was not her husband, as he was in Europe with the advancing Allied armies. Her skirt was halfway up her thigh.

Sensing our presence, she looked up angrily. We had startled her and no doubt embarrassed her, and she was furious. 'Get out! Get away!' she cried out.

We turned and ran back to the front of the house and along the road to the footpath leading through Stokes Farm. It was the first time that we had come across infidelity and we were shocked. Instinctively we knew that it was wrong. Every adult couple we knew – Mum and Dad, Mr and Mrs Ferris, our aunts and uncles, Betty and Margaret's parents and all the shopkeepers in the parade of shops where we lived – were faithfully married, so far as we knew. That was the way it was, or at least appeared to be in our world, and any deviation from it was unthinkable, although in retrospect, I realise now that one or two of the people we knew may have been unfaithful.

An hour later, we found the front door unlocked when we got back to the house. We crept upstairs quietly and waited for Mum to arrive, but we were too shocked – and perhaps too embarrassed – to mention it to her.

# 17

# A MIXED BAG

While we were still in Chalfont, we learnt from the radio one morning that in France the Germans were holding up the British advance at a city named Caen, the centre of which was almost totally destroyed in the ensuing fighting, with thousands of civilians killed or wounded. Then, a week or so later, the city was captured, and the Allied forces fanned out across northern France.

Faced with this new reality, many German generals realised that the war was lost, as a result of the Russians pushing in from the east, and the Western Allies advancing towards Germany from the west and also progressing northwards up the length of Italy. In July 1944, some of the generals were part of a plot to assassinate Hitler. Hundreds of thousands – possibly even a million or so – Allied and German lives might have been saved if they had succeeded, or others had been able to persuade Hitler to surrender. But surrender was not in the Führer's or the Nazis' psyche. Right to the end of war, he and they hung on the belief that, by some as yet unrealised miracle, they could win the war. Even when the fighting spread to Germany, they continued to fight on, although it would lead to the destruction and impoverishment of their own country.

★★★

When the school in Amersham closed for the summer holidays, Richard and I left Chalfont and went with Mum and Dad to a farm near Taunton in Somerset to have a holiday and continue to escape the V bombs that were still raining down on London. Because of the invasion of Europe, all the trains in the south of England had been commandeered by the armed services. The only way we could get to Taunton was by travelling by train at night and changing trains several times, with the result that we didn't arrive there until six o'clock the next morning. As the train was finally approaching Taunton station, a young American soldier, who was sitting opposite us and travelling on the train with his British girlfriend, leaned forward and gave Richard and me some chewing gum and a couple of bars of chocolate and presented Dad with a big cigar. Outside the station, the town was still asleep, but eventually we found a café, although even by the standards of the war, the breakfast we were served was inedible, consisting of pieces of burnt toast, eggs that were fried until they were like plastic, and strips of white pork fat that were passed off as bacon.

The farm where we stayed was close to the small hamlet of West Hatch and was run by a young woman named Mrs Heal whose husband was away at the war. This was before many of the hedges in the country had been cut down to create larger fields, and the countryside was still a patchwork of small fields, each no larger than a few acres. A brook ran under the farmhouse, which was several hundred years old. Living on a farm was an idyllic experience for children brought up in a city during a war. There was as much farm-produced fresh butter, chicken, eggs, fruit and milk as we could eat. Swallows nested under the eaves of the buildings. Each morning I went out to the barn that served as a chicken coop and put my hand through a series of small holes at the back of the line of chicken boxes to collect any eggs that had been laid overnight.

Because farm labour was in short supply, Dad suggested that it would be a good idea if the family volunteered to work on the farm – or on a nearby farm – and so the whole family, including Mum and us two boys, helped harvest several fields of the flax used for making linen. It was hard, gruelling work under a hot summer sun. As cutting the crop would have shortened the fibres from which linen was made, each plant had to be pulled whole by hand in one piece from the ground, and our hands were soon very red and sore and our backs aching from bending repeatedly. For an adult, the pay for a day's grinding work was about 12s, or 60p in today's money; for children, such as Richard and me, it was about a couple of shillings, or 10p in today's terms.

When we got home from our holiday, Dad told Mum that while we were away he had received a telegram informing him that Mum's dad, Grandpa Morris, had died suddenly while having his afternoon nap in his chair. When she heard the news, Mum was furious with Dad and asked by what right he had kept the news from her. Why hadn't he informed her of it as soon as he received the telegram? Dad's answer was that he was trying to protect her and wanted her to rest and have an enjoyable holiday while we were away. But Mum wasn't satisfied and repeated that Dad had taken a decision that he hadn't any right to take, and for several days afterwards the atmosphere between them was soured. I don't remember how I reacted to Grandpa Morris's death; I can only surmise that for reasons I cannot recall it did not affect me as deeply as Grandpa Model's death had done.

★★★

To continue escaping the V bombs, a day or so after returning from Somerset, Richard and I were taken by train with Mum and Dad to stay with the Ferrises, who, to escape the bombs, had moved to a small bungalow in the hamlet of Rushmore, near Farnham in Surrey, about 40 miles south of London. Having delivered us, Mum and Dad returned to London, but joined us at weekends.

The Ferrises had picked a beautiful part of Surrey in which to live. Like Chalfont, Rushmore was an idyllic place for two boys to be temporarily evacuated. Backing onto the Ferrises' new home was an area of heathland and fir forest that no one other than a few local people knew of. With Rita, we passed long summer days exploring it and the surrounding countryside.

We were there in August and the heather was in bloom, with the land carpeted in tiny purple flowers. In among the heather were two lakes, and on one side of the area was a steep hill from the summit of which we could look out over the surrounding hills and forests as far as the Devil's Punchbowl away to the south. While we were roaming, we climbed several fir trees, and in one tree built a plat-form made of branches that we had cut down.

A small area of the heath had been fenced off by the RAF as an experimental bombing range for testing small bombs delivered by parachute. The fence round the area was about 8ft high, and attached to it were notices saying 'Air Ministry Property. Danger. Keep Out. Live ammunition. Trespassers will be prosecuted'.

Mr Ferris told us that the RAF would not practise with live ammunition so near people's homes. A few days later, when we were out on a walk, we saw a metal cylinder about 2ft long on the inner side of the fence. Attached to it was a small, white silk parachute.

We peered at it through the criss-cross wires of the fence. The parachute looked very tempting.

'It's one of their dummy bombs. I think we should get that parachute,' Richard said.

Rita and I weren't so sure. 'It might be dangerous. We'd need to get through the fence,' I said doubtfully.

'I don't want to have anything more to do with it. I'm going home,' Rita said snootily, and walked off.

'Well, don't tell your Mum and Dad about it,' I called after her.

Reluctantly, I followed Richard along the fence.

About 50 yards from the cylinder was a hole under the fence, presumably dug by an animal such as a fox.

'We can get a branch and make the hole bigger, and get in there!' Richard said.

Ten minutes later, we were on the other side of the fence, and crouching low, crept towards the cylinder while at the same time keeping a lookout for anyone who might spot us.

The cylinder or practice bomb was lying on the heather. The parachute looked to be about 2ft in diameter, was attached to the cylinder by silk strings and was fastened to it with nuts and bolts.

I was very nervous and jittery. 'We'd better be quick. Don't disturb it. We don't want it to explode,' I said.

The nuts were easily undone with our fingers, and about a minute or so later Richard picked up the parachute and we hoofed it back to the hole and the other side of the fence as quickly as we could.

Fortunately, the soil we had crawled over to get through the hole was sand, and so we were easily able to rub it off our clothes as we walked back to the Ferrises' home.

A day or so later, we went back and got another parachute, so that we each had one, and as we did so we saw that the cylinder from which we had taken the first parachute had been removed.

Our final caper while we were at the Ferrises' was to buy some cigarettes, or at least try to buy some, as the three of us, that is Rita and we boys, suddenly fancied trying a smoke. As I was the oldest and tallest, I was chosen to go to the one and only local shop and do my best. I rehearsed what I was going to say, and decided not to ask for Woodbines, which were the cheapest cigarettes on the market, as I thought the shopkeeper would suspect I was buying them for myself. Instead, the three of us had agreed before I left for the shop that I should ask the shopkeeper for Player's or Black Cat cigarettes.

'What can I do for you?' the man behind the counter asked, as I walked into the shop.

'Ten Black Cat cigarettes, please,' I said as casually as I could, expecting to be challenged.

I watched as the shopkeeper reached behind him without saying a word, and then, in exchange for a shilling, hand me a packet of ten Black Cat cigarettes.

I got out of the shop as quickly as I could. As soon as I was back at the Ferrises', the three of us retired to a wooden shed in their garden and lit up. But it was not a success. Smoking made us nauseous and giddy and left us feeling very unwell.

★★★

In September, after a month at Rushmore, Richard and I returned to London with our parachutes, and I went back to John Lyon School. As I walked up the road from South Harrow station to the school one morning, I saw that the sky was covered in Dakota aircraft, each slowly towing a glider full of what I guessed were soldiers and equipment. To my young eyes, the planes and gliders looked like huge black insects crawling slowly across the sky. They were flying so low that I could see the towlines between the aircraft and the gliders, and there were so many of them that it looked as if they were part of an enormous canopy covering the whole sky. Later, I realised that the ones I saw were one of three huge columns, each of which had taken off from a different airfield. Walking silently beneath them, as they lumbered on, I was aware that they were likely to be on their way to a terrible battle and that many of the young men inside them were likely to be dead by the time I came out of school, and I feared for them. Later, I learnt from the radio or Dad's newspaper that they were British paratroopers who were part of an operation named Market Garden, and they were on their way to a town named Arnhem in the Netherlands, where it was hoped they would facilitate the advance of the Allied armies into Germany by capturing several vital bridges over the River Rhine. But it was not to be. Unbeknown to them or the Allied generals commanding them, a large formation of German Panzer tanks was resting nearby, commanded by my namesake Field Marshal Model, one of Hitler's favourite generals – but, I hasten to add, no relation of mine! The lightly armed paratroopers fought heroically for a week against overwhelming odds and hung on to the bridges for several days longer than might have been expected, but in the end over half of them were killed, captured or wounded, and the bridges remained in German hands for the time being.

Just before Christmas 1944, I heard on the radio that the Germans had launched a surprise attack with tanks through the Ardennes, a hilly, forested area where Belgium, France and Luxembourg meet. Their aim was to destroy several Allied armies and prevent them using the port of Antwerp to bring in supplies. Fortunately they failed, but not before young, lightly armed American soldiers had helped to halt their advance at a town named Bastogne. While the battle for the town was raging, the German commander sent a message to the American commander, Brigadier General Anthony McAuliffe, suggesting that, in order to save lives, he and his troops should surrender, to which General McAuliffe famously replied 'Nuts!' But the cost of the resistance implied by the reply was high. Some 19,000 Americans were killed during the Battle of the Bulge, as the battle became known. On the German side, tens of thousands of men eventually lost their lives by the time the battle was over.

Twenty-five years later, a friend and I were motoring through the Ardennes on our way to holiday in Florence and other parts of Italy. By chance, our route took us through Bastogne. To our surprise, the town seemed to be deserted. Then, in the distance, we heard the sound of a lone bugle, and made our way towards it. The local people had not forgotten the American sacrifice. Twenty-five years after the war, the whole population of the town had assembled in the town square and were attending a service of remembrance for the young American soldiers who gave their lives in defence of their town more than two decades previously.

★★★

Christmas 1944 was dominated by the death and destruction occurring in Europe and the continuing V1 and V2 attacks on the south of England, and London in particular. The weather was freezing cold. Central heating was almost unknown in Britain at that time. At home, we were cold, despite heavy curtains at the windows and bolsters at the bottom of the doors to keep draughts out. The only part of a room likely to be warm was near a source of heat, and people huddled close to coal fires and paraffin stoves.

Our family, plus Bingo, spent Christmas and Boxing Day with the Ferrises in their bungalow in Rushmore. Mr Ferris killed a couple of the ducks he kept and we had a good Christmas lunch. After lunch we huddled round a log fire in the Ferrises' sitting room and listened on the radio to our much-loved king stutter his way through his Christmas speech.

On Boxing Day morning Rita, Richard and I went for a walk, to see if the lake in the centre of the heath behind the Ferrises' home was frozen. The bombing range had gone and the heathland was hard with frost. The lake was frozen with ice several inches deep. With typical daring, before Rita and I could stop him, Richard struck out to walk across the ice. After perhaps 30 yards of slithering and sliding and trying to keep his balance, Rita and I heard the ice crack, and a moment later saw a hole appear in it and water ripple up out of it, as Richard sank into it. Fortunately, our parents weren't with us. But for the fact that the water was only about 3ft deep, Richard might have sunk beneath the ice and been drowned. As it was, he ended up standing up to his waist in ice-cold water. For a few moments he clambered about in an effort to heave himself out onto intact ice, then, after calming down and moving more slowly, he succeeded in slithering out and eventually joined us at the lakeside. He was wet and shivering with the cold. His lower half was soaking and dripping icy water and, as we walked back to the Ferrises', ice-cold water squelched from the sides of his boots. When Dad saw him, he gave a shocked laugh, then told him off and helped him out of his clothes and towelled him down.

★★★

By January 1945 it was obvious that something was happening to Mum. She wasn't just comfortably plump and mumsy to cuddle. She was visibly larger.

At breakfast one day, Richard said to her, 'Mum! Your tummy's getting bigger and bigger!' as she turned in the kitchen and we saw her in profile.

Dad put his newspaper down, and said, 'Your Mum's going to have a baby. What do you think about that?'

In unison, we replied that we would love to have a new member of the family, but it had better be a boy, so we could build our own football team.

'Wouldn't you like a little sister?' Dad asked, voicing the outcome that both he and Mum hoped for.

'The whole family's boys. Even Bingo's a boy,' I said.

Mum and Dad laughed.

'Well, we'll have to wait and see,' Mum said. 'Your Dad and I would like a little girl.'

On 3 February Mum developed abdominal pains, and Dad phoned for a taxi to take the two of them to the nursing home in which Richard and I had been born near the bottom of Hampstead Heath.

As Mum was leaving, one of us boys – I don't remember which – was pretty blunt about the outcome we desired of the birth and, in what was to become a family joke, said, 'Don't bother to come home if it's a girl!'

Mum laughed, then winced with pain, and a few moments later they left.

The following day she gave birth to a little boy, whom she and Dad named David.

On the Sunday that Mum was away, Dad cooked a lunch of roast leg of lamb for us. But although almost everything about it was the way it should have been, it just wasn't the same as when Mum cooked it. For one thing, it didn't taste the same. It looked the same, but it just wasn't. For another, Dad forgot to make any gravy, and instead of getting one of us boys to lay the table, simply put a pile of knives and forks in the middle of the table for us to take and use as we wished. But we didn't complain. As decent little chaps, we made the appropriate foody noises as we ate our dry roast potatoes and overheated baked beans, and slipped Bingo the odd piece of roast lamb.

The first thing David did, when he arrived home with Mum from the nursing home, was to cry to be fed in the high-pitched way that newborn babies do.

For a moment, Mum hesitated. 'Perhaps the boys should go out while I feed David?' she said to Dad, as we sat round the kitchen table.

A moment of silence ensued, then Dad said, 'Feeding a baby is natural. I think the boys should see how David is fed.'

Mum agreed, and we watched as she undid the buttons on her blouse and slipped out her breast for David to attach himself to. After that, we didn't notice when he was being fed.

David soon endeared himself to us and earned a big place in the family. We referred to him as the Buzz Bomb Baby. We particularly liked the way that, when he was about a year old, he roared for his food as he sat in his highchair at the corner of the kitchen table.

# 18

# VICTORY, BUT NOT THE END OF THE WAR

On 21 March 1945, the last V1s and V2s were fired at Britain. Realising that the Germans had lost the war, and that Hitler's orders to the German Army to fight to the last man were the words of a madman, Field Marshal Walter Model ordered the 300,000 soldiers under his command to disband and return to their homes; then in despair, he opened the door of his quarters, went out into the forest and shot himself.

★★★

One morning in April 1945, just after Richard and I had come down to breakfast, Dad opened *The Daily Telegraph*, took one look at the pictures and the news item accompanying them and put down his paper. With tears in his eyes, he quietly excused himself and left the kitchen to go into the adjoining front room. As soon as the door had closed behind him, Richard and I picked up the paper and saw what he had just seen. The pictures were the first evidence to be seen by the public in the West of yet another bestial aspect of Nazism. Dad was shocked because he could not believe that the country of his forebears – the country that had produced Mozart, Beethoven and Goethe – could have been responsible for what he had seen in the newspaper. Splashed across its pages, and across cinema screens of the time, were scenes that no human being should have to see, let alone live through.

As they fought their way across northern Germany, British troops came across an unknown concentration camp near the town of Bergen. In the camp, known as Bergen-Belsen, they found 60,000 starving people, suffering from diseases such as typhoid, typhus, tuberculosis

The children of Auschwitz. (Alexander Vorontsov/Galerie Bilderwelt/ Getty Images)

Rows of dead bodies at Belsen Concentration Camp. (Everett Collection Historical/Alamy)

and dysentery. Thirteen thousand decomposing bodies were lying about, some of them in heaps. The childhood diarist Anne Frank had been murdered there. The abiding memory I still have of the films and photos I saw at that time is of skeletal-like people dressed in clothes that looked like striped pyjamas, standing with uncomprehending, deep, cavernous eyes in the doorway of a wooden barrack outside of which similarly dressed bodies lay dead on the ground. Another memory I have of Belsen is of a large pile of bodies being bulldozed into a mass grave. No wonder then that I am sensitive about the implications of being partly Jewish. Is this what could have been done to me? The local German dignitaries from the town of Bergen lied and denied all knowledge of the place when they were brought to witness what their nation had done.

***

The Germans continued to fight on despite the hopelessness of their situation. Appreciating that the game was up, on 30 April 1945 Hitler committed suicide in his bunker under the Reichstag, and Admiral Dönitz became head of what remained of the German state. In the cinema I saw Pathé News film of Russian troops hoisting the red Russian flag over the Reichstag. On 7 May, German forces officially surrendered. Over the following days, the people of Britain, and all over Europe, went wild celebrating. There was a sense of unreality about it. War had become the way we lived and it was difficult to comprehend that it was over. Vast crowds gathered in central London. At Buckingham Palace, King George VI and Queen Elizabeth (later to become the Queen Mother) greeted the people from the balcony at the front of the palace, accompanied by the two princesses, Princess Elizabeth (later to be Queen Elizabeth II) and her younger sister, Princess Margaret. Mr Churchill, who more than any other person had inspired the British people to persevere until victory was achieved, joined them on the balcony to pay tribute to the crowd.

All over the country, people rejoiced and arranged street parties. Bunting was hung out. Union Jacks were draped across buildings, or flew proudly from flagpoles. Fortunately, the weather was dry. At some street parties people sang and danced in the street, and girls wore paper hats carrying messages such as, 'Kiss me quick'. At other street parties, men dressed formally in suits; while at others still, games such as tug of war and egg-and-spoon races were played. In Wembley, Richard and I were given tiny Union Jacks on short sticks that we waved whenever anyone spoke to us. We helped Dad drape red, white and blue bunting across the front of the shop and hang a large Union Jack from one of the windows of the flat. In Eagle Road, the side road beside the shop, tables were erected in the middle of the street. A special table for children was prepared. Food might still be rationed, but plates of sandwiches, cakes and sausage rolls were produced and the tables were laden with food. Apple tart and custard, jelly and blancmange were served as dessert. Jugs of squash and several bottles of Tizer, the sweet fizzy drink, were placed on the children's table. Tizer was popular at the time but, because of its cost, Richard and I were only allowed it on special occasions. On one or two tables, there were even a few bottles of beer. All the kids from our street – Richard and me, Betty and Margaret, John and Rene Curtis, my friend Lawrence, Graham and Margaret Dobson, and a few kids from further up the street – waited expectantly for five o'clock and the party to begin.

Some grown-ups at the party were full of bonhomie. Others were a bit shy. Mum and Dad looked strange sitting at a table in the middle of the road some 20 yards from us, eating and chatting quietly to several neighbours. It was the first time that Betty and Margaret's dad, Mr Bradford, had ever been seen outside the grocers he managed next door to our home. As a consequence, he had not been exposed to the sun, and his face was so white that he looked positively ill. On a table further up the street, John and Rene Curtis's dad, the dignified train driver, sat comfortably smoking his pipe. Beside him, Mrs Curtis was still wearing an apron, but it had been freshly washed and ironed, and added colour to her otherwise drab dress. Other people whom I met only occasionally in the street, were at the party. Mr Barker, the 80-year-old owner of a big store in Wembley High Road, was there, as was another elderly man who was accompanied by his bachelor son, a fireman, who still lived at home with his dad despite being in his middle 40s.

There was also another somewhat strange middle-aged man at the party. Each weekday morning on my way to school, I saw him swaggering down the road, wearing an early form of jeans jacket and baseball cap. Who did he think he was, I wondered? Who was he trying to imitate? Did he think he was some kind of American folk hero?

At our table, we kids ate ourselves full of sausage rolls, cakes, apple pie, trifle and jelly and blancmange, washed down with Tizer.

At eight o'clock, a few grown-ups discreetly drifted away, and others began to look about them. At our table,

Photo of Street party in Barrow. (Via southlakes-uk.co.uk and Bill Clarke, CCA 4.0)

no food remained. At nine o'clock, a few more people left, and by eleven o'clock it was all over. Everyone had had a good time.

★★★

But the war was not over. While Britain and the people of Europe went wild and celebrated the defeat of Nazi Germany, on the far side of the world the Allies were still engaged in bitter fighting with the Japanese. As Cousin Gordon did not speak about what happened to him after the Battle of Kohima, I have no idea whether he was still involved in the fighting, or whether he was suffering from shellshock and unfit to do so.

In the cinema I saw newsreel showing that the Japanese were fighting as savagely as ever in Burma, and that the Fourteenth Army – known as the Lost Army because it got so little press coverage – was still sustaining heavy casualties as its soldiers fought an enemy who would rather die than surrender. The newsreels also showed film of British soldiers in Burma halfway up to their chests in water, with their rifles held above their heads, as they struggled to cross fast-flowing rivers swollen by monsoon rains.

From Pathé News, I learnt that further east, in the Pacific, the Americans were having to fight from island to island in order to get to Japan and finish the war. In the battle for the Philippine Islands more than 20,000 young Americans were killed and an unbelievable 340,000 young Japanese, either in the fighting, from starvation or by committing suicide rather than surrendering. Unacceptable as these figures are, they pale beside the 100,000 citizens of Manila who were killed, many massacred by the Japanese.

Similar casualties were sustained in each of the battles for the Japanese islands of Iwo Jima and Okinawa. In fascinated horror, I watched newsreel showing Japanese women gathering on the cliffs of Okinawa and throwing their babies and then themselves onto the rocks or into the sea below in the belief that if they fell into American hands they would be tortured, raped and killed. I wondered how they could believe that, as to me the Americans were our friends and allies. What I didn't know was that the Japanese people were being conditioned to fight to the death, rather than surrender their homeland.

★★★

A few days after Okinawa fell to the Americans, on the other side of the world Britain became embroiled in a general election. Mum and Dad supported the Liberal Party. In the days preceding the election, Mrs Gray co-opted Richard and me to work as unpaid Liberal Party workers distributing hundreds of yellow pamphlets through the letter boxes of homes in the part of Wembley in which we lived.

In view of his record as our wartime leader, and the leading part he had played in the defeat of Nazi Germany, it was generally expected that Mr Churchill's Conservative Party would win. But the people of Britain were tired of war and wanted a change. Many associated Mr Churchill with the war, and so, to everyone's surprise, Labour was voted in in a landslide victory. As a result, an almost unknown, quiet man named Clement Attlee, who lacked charisma but as leader of the Labour Party had been deputy prime minister during the war, became our prime minister in the last stages of the conflict, and went on to be one of the most effective reforming prime ministers the country has ever had.

As you might expect, most of the masters and boys at John Lyon School were in despair immediately after the election, to be followed by a sneering acceptance of what had happened, as they were Conservative to a man – or almost so. There were a few exceptions. Influenced by his father, my friend Gerald Godfrey declared himself to be a socialist and Labour supporter.

★★★

Back on the other side the world, the Allies were reluctant to sustain further casualties and issued an ultimatum to the Japanese, threatening 'prompt and utter' destruction of the armed forces and homeland if the Japanese failed to accept unconditional surrender. They rejected the ultimatum and the next thing we heard was that, in order to shorten the war and save lives, rightly or wrongly, on 6 August 1945 the Americans dropped a newly developed weapon – the atom bomb – on Hiroshima. Estimates of the number of people killed by the bomb vary widely, but were in the vicinity of 100,000, with another 100,000 wounded. As the Japanese still failed to surrender, on 9 August a second atom bomb was dropped on the city of Nagasaki, causing slightly fewer casualties to those sustained at Hiroshima. At noon on 15 August, Emperor Hirohito of Japan – whom the Japanese people had never seen or heard, as he was revered as a god who lived in isolation in his palace in Tokyo – broadcast to his nation for the first time, saying, 'We have resolved to pave the way for a grand peace for

all the generations to come by enduring the unendurable
and suffering what is insufferable.'

★★★

News of the Japanese surrender caused an upsurge of celebrations across the world. In Britain, large crowds gathered
in the streets, squares, parks and plazas. In London, the
celebrations coincided with the opening of Parliament,
and huge crowds gathered to celebrate victory and to
watch the king and queen pass by in an open carriage on
their way to open Parliament by way of the Mall, Trafalgar
Square and Whitehall. Later that day, the new prime minister, Mr Attlee, broadcast to the nation in a speech in
which he said, 'The last of our enemies is laid low …'

In Wembley, bunting was hung out and Union Jacks
were flown again. Once again, Richard and I helped Dad
drape the same red, white and blue bunting between the
window of the flat in Mum and Dad's bedroom and the
window in the front room, and fly the same Union Jack as
we had done when the Germans surrendered.

★★★

The formal surrender of Japan did not happen until a
week after the emperor's speech. On 22 September 1945,
in scenes that were flashed across the world in photo and
film, General MacArthur for the Allies and a delegation
from Japan, signed the surrender document on the deck
of the United States battleship USS *Missouri* in Tokyo Bay.
Thus, the Second World War, the bloodiest war in history,
came to a formal end.

The formal surrender of Japan on board the USS *Missouri*. (Naval Historical Center Photo # USA C-2719, Army Signal Corps Collection in the US National Archives)

★★★

At John Lyon School, the boys and the masters informally debated whether dropping the atomic bombs to shorten the war and save lives was justified or was a crime against humanity. Opinions were divided, although most of my friends and I thought that dropping the bombs and forcing the Japanese to surrender probably saved tens of thousands of Allied lives and hundreds of thousands – or possibly a million or more – Japanese lives.

# 19

# EIGHTY YEARS ON

Eighteen months after the end of the war, Mum's tummy swelled once again and, despite Mum and Dad's wish for a baby girl, on 31 August my brother Martin was born, much to the relief of Richard and me, who, as you may guess, advised Mum not to return home if the baby was a girl.

Cousins Gordon and Maurice were demobilised from the army shortly after the end of the war, and went into business together. They opened a large store selling men's clothes in Baker Street, London. Shortly afterwards, Gordon married and settled down happily, although he remained unwell for several years as a result of his experiences fighting the Japanese in Burma.

During the war, people from very different backgrounds were forced to mix and after the war cracks began to appear in the country's rigid class structure. Slowly but surely, society was becoming more egalitarian and less class-bound than it had been before the war. By the time he was discharged from the army, the son of our local baker had risen to the rank of captain and, feigning a modesty I am sure he did not feel, wore his officer's uniform while selling bread in his mother's shop for the first few days after he was demobbed so he could show how well he had done in the service of his country. By the same token, for a few days, the son of Mum's preferred grocer, Elborns, wore his major's uniform in his parents' shop. He was wearing it when he served me the list of groceries Mum had sent me to get.

In the wider world, Britain and her allies might have won the war, but winning it had left the country exhausted and almost bankrupt. No longer was Britain top dog. At the end of the war, the country had a very good army, the second largest navy in the world and an air force that was second to none. But the reality was that all the country's money had been spent on waging the war and manufacturing war materials. Food was still rationed and would remain so until 1953, eight years after the end of the war. The street lights might have been switched on, but the lights in Piccadilly Circus had not, and would not be until 1949. In Wembley, a pre-war idiosyncrasy in the street lighting persisted for several years after the end of the war. Although most of the street lights where I lived were electric, a single street lamp close to my home was powered by gas, and was lit every evening and extinguished every morning by a man who arrived on a bicycle with a short ladder on his shoulder that he ascended to switch the light on or off.

In human terms, the war had cost Britain dearly. Some 384,000 of its finest young men and women in the armed forces, and 67,000 of its civilians, had been killed. The British Empire, the largest empire the world had ever seen, was about to be dissolved. Although the empire was so large that it was said that the sun was always shining on some part of it, the people on whom that sun shone were restive and, not unreasonably, wanted freedom to rule themselves, even if in practice in some cases it led to corruption and tyranny. Within thirty years the empire had gone, to be replaced by the Commonwealth, a voluntary association of fifty-four nations. Within fifty years of the war, many young Britons would hardly know that the empire had existed.

★★★

America was now top dog and was triumphant in every respect. It had the size and natural resources that Britain did not have. Its industries had flourished during the war. Twenty-five years previously, the Royal Navy had been the largest and most powerful in the world. Now the US Navy, as well as its army and air force, were far larger than Britain's. America was the greatest industrial power on Earth and under the 1948 Marshall Plan exported goods and money to every part of the world in order to help the reconstruction of countries that had been ravaged by the war. It was generous enough not to require repayment, although Britain did repay other loans made by America.

The other great powers that had helped to win the war were Russia and China. Both were dictatorships. Many of the largest battles of the Second World War had been fought in Russia, and defeating Nazi Germany had cost it dearly. Twenty-five million Russians had been killed. Its ruler, Stalin, was paranoid and was responsible for the deaths of many other Russians, with estimates varying between 9 and 20 million people. The Russian Red Army was the biggest in the world at the end of the war, and occupied and suppressed the countries of Eastern Europe in a move that Mr Churchill described in a speech to the American Senate as an 'iron curtain' being lowered across Europe to separate and prevent communication between the people of Russia and Eastern Europe on the one hand, and people of the Western democracies on the other.

The greatest paradox of the post-war period was that each of the two most powerful victors of the war, namely Russia and the United States, believed that the other wished to annihilate it. The Russians believed that they might be attacked by America and the Americans believed that they might be attacked by the Russians. Hence the threat of nuclear annihilation and the stand-off known as the Cold War.

Both Russia and China professed to be communist states but, like Russia, China was really a one-party state ruled by a dictator. The ill-conceived policies of Mao Zedong known as the Great Leap Forward and the Cultural Revolution were responsible for millions of deaths, possibly as high as 45 million people. Economically, the rigid centrally directed Russian and Chinese economies were no match for the flexible free enterprise economies of the Western democracies. But the Western economies are not without their problems. Free enterprise and democracy are essentially about empowering individuals and enabling them to realise their full potential, if they wish to do so. But individuals are by nature acquisitive, and over the years some members of democratic societies have acquired more and more wealth. That has led to societies in which there is great inequality, with people having much more money than they can possibly spend or need in their lifetimes, while millions and millions of other people are poor and don't have enough. No doubt the very rich feel that their wealth gives them power and security, but to me it seems they have lost their sense of proportion and don't understand that they – along with the rest of us – are merely visitors here on Earth. They don't appreciate that life is finite and lasts for only a few short years, and you cannot take your goods and money with you when you die.

How societies deal with these problems, and the problems posed by climate change, the digital revolution and overpopulation are the great challenges facing mankind in the twenty-first century. Whether humankind has the capacity to resolve these problems remains to be seen, as its curiosity and ability to invent and make things far outweighs its wisdom and ability to co-operate.

★★★

Despite the change in Britain's role in the world, life in austerity Britain after the war could be happy if you lived in a happy family and a close relative had not been killed or maimed in the conflict. The country might not be top dog anymore, and might be searching for a new role in the world, but it had a new government that was working for the people and was about to launch the Welfare State and the National Health Service (NHS), a health system that promised free access to health care for all. London, the city in which I lived, might have suffered badly during the war, and might be shabby, in need of reconstruction and subject to rationing, but the importance of those things was relative, as it is relationships that contribute most to people's happiness. I was lucky, as I came from a happy family in which Mum loved Dad, Dad loved Mum, and both loved us boys. Money might have been tight, but Mum and Dad ensured that we got the best education they could afford, and so I was optimistic about my future.

Of course, I had my difficulties. For young people, the 1950s was very different to today. Apart from the Bobby-soxers in the United States, there was no youth culture. The young were merely mirrors of the adults they knew. They dressed in similar ways and, apart from being more adventurous and probably more curious in the way that young animals are, they behaved in similar ways. I was interested in girls but was shy and lacked confidence where they were concerned. My body was pumping out hormones in a way that it would never quite do again, shouting at my mind that it wanted to have sex. But I was forbidden to do so.

There was no sex education. One day when I was 15, Dad said to me, 'Don't do anything that you might regret.' And that was it, my sex education in seven words. Premarital sex was forbidden, and so was impossible for someone brought up strictly like me. Mum and Dad made it clear that they expected my brothers and me to remain chaste and to be virgins when we married. If you disobeyed expectations and by chance made a girl pregnant, you were expected to marry her. Unlike today, unmarried mothers were shunned and lived in disgrace. Just three things kept me on the straight and narrow: the fear of risking myself and launching into something about which I knew nothing; the fear and consequences of making a girl pregnant; and the fear of getting a sexual disease such as gonorrhoea or syphilis. Fortunately, today attitudes to sexual relationships are much healthier. The change occurred in the 1960s and was due to three main factors: the gradual easing of attitudes in general throughout society in the '50s; the sudden independence of young people, who for the first time in history had more money than they required for the immediate necessities of life; and the invention of the contraceptive pill, which relieved them of the worry of pregnancy.

★★★

For as long as I can remember, my ambition was to be an officer in the Royal Navy. But on the advice of a golfing friend of Dad's, who was a senior executive at Shell, I opted instead to join the Merchant Navy. In 1949, I enrolled as a cadet on the Spartan Merchant Navy training ship HMS *Worcester*, moored at Greenhithe, near the mouth of the River Thames, and was instructed in the art of seamanship and navigation. Aged 18, I went to sea as a cadet, and then as an officer, in the Shaw Savill Shipping Company, running mainly to Australia and New Zealand, although I visited many other parts of the world. It was a youth like almost no other, the golden era of seafaring, before globalisation and modern communications, and before McDonald's and Hilton had reduced many places to a mid-Atlantic norm. When I was at sea, each country I visited was still more or less the way it had been for many decades. Containerisation of cargoes and the fast turn-round of ships had not yet been invented, and the ships I served on were in port for days or weeks at a time, so I was able to explore the countries I went to.

Perhaps as a result of my travels, while I was at sea I began to question who I was. I was still bothered by the fact that I wasn't sure whether or not I was Jewish. I knew that Mum was Jewish but I still wasn't sure if that meant I was Jewish. As previously mentioned, because religion had caused so much trouble in each of their families, Mum and Dad had chosen not to discuss religion with Richard and me. At school, I did not know how to respond to the occasional antisemitic taunt directed at me. Was I a Jew or not? That might not matter much in today's multicultural world, but it mattered a great deal in the antisemitic world of the 1950s in which Jews were barred from many clubs and institutions throughout Britain.

Like many sensitive young people, I was in turmoil, a mixture of ambitions, hopes and insecurities: who am I? How should I live my life? What will happen to me after I die? Is there or is there not an afterlife? For three years I tried to answer these questions and find a place for myself in the world by reading widely and labouring over books such as the Bible, Descartes's *Discourse on the Method* and Spinoza's *Ethics*, as well as books about Buddhism, Islam and Freud.

Without being aware of it, like many teenagers I reacted to my insecurities with a veneer of invincibility and so I became a macho man. Now I know that being macho was nothing more than a pose and a way of compensating for the doubts and insecurities of which I was unaware. For some years I thought of myself as a tough guy and, even though I did not act tough, I thought tough. Then eventually, I realised that what I was doing was nothing more than an act. 'Come off it, Doug,' I said to myself. 'Your macho pose is pathetic. You know better than that. Real men don't pretend to be tough; they are gentle and kind, and don't adopt a pose, but embrace life as it really is.' Even so, I recognise a trace of macho man in me still, despite the fact that I am now well into my 80s.

After several years at sea, I realised that it wasn't a career I wished to pursue for the rest of my life, as I saw that the life of the captain on a large merchant ship was usually very isolated. Also, to my surprise, I discovered that I wanted to pursue an occupation that was more academic, and I wanted to be able to devote myself in a more personal way to the service of the public and society. But it wasn't easy to find a career that would fulfil my wishes. For a while I cast around not knowing what to do, and was worried and irritable and unable to sleep. I felt trapped by indecision. Among the ideas I toyed with was becoming a school teacher, but it didn't seem to be academic enough. Then, I lighted upon the idea of trying to become a doctor. It seemed an impossible wish that I, a man of the sea who knew only about ships, navigation and cargoes, might pursue such a career. For one thing, I did not have any A levels, the modern prerequisite for getting into university. For another, I wasn't helped by the opinion of people I knew. In short order, I was told that I was too old to undertake such a calling and that, in any case, because of the competition to get into medical school, I would not get a place. Despite such discouragement, I applied, and was lucky enough to be accepted. But first I needed to save some money and to complete my career at sea, and so I waited until I was able to take the exams that would qualify me to be the master or captain of a large ship, and am as proud of my Master's Certificate as I am of my medical degrees.

After medical school, I opted for a career in hospital medicine and eventually, after marrying a lovely specialist nurse named Jillie, became a happily married consultant physician working in a large hospital that served over a quarter of a million people in Eastbourne in East Sussex. But although I have been a doctor for more than fifty years and think like a doctor, because I was at sea during the formative years of my life, I still think of myself as a seaman as well. As I walk along the street, the doctor in me instinctively looks at the people I pass to see if I can see any physical signs that point to a diagnosis, but at the same time, the sailor in me looks up at the sky and notes the height and type of the clouds and the direction of the wind and whether there is likely to be any rain.

Dad, my mentor, my best friend, the man who taught me how to love, who shaped my conscience and from whom I obtained my values, died suddenly at the relatively young age of 52. Some months before his death, he intimated that he felt he had been a failure. After the war he had gone back to ladies' hairdressing, but he hated it and stuck it for only a few years. After that he worked around the home, building two garages on top of our old air-raid shelter and a room with two dormer windows in the loft above our flat. He also helped Mum with the shop, but it wasn't a proper career. He had an academic brain and felt that he had not fulfilled his potential, which bothered him. But he had been happily married and had raised four law-abiding boys and, speaking for myself, I am aware of his presence every day. He lives on in me. I have his genes and often feel that I am the living embodiment of him and am seeing the world through his eyes. So perhaps he was more successful than he thought?

Because, physically, he was such a strong man, his death was a great shock to our neighbours and everyone in our family. I found it difficult to comprehend how someone normally so healthy could die within a few hours of becoming unwell, and was so upset that I cried and cried and cried my eyes out.

Mum continued to run the shop until she retired in her middle 60s. Richard grew up, married and became the owner of a highly successful business selling office equipment. Mr and Mrs Ferris and Rita emigrated to New Zealand shortly after the war. Lawrence and his parents emigrated to Western Australia in the middle of the 1950s. Seventy years on, I still keep in regular contact by phone with both Rita and Lawrence.

Wembley changed. Over the years, more and more people from Asia have moved in, and now 90 per cent of the population is from India and Pakistan. The other 10 per cent is mainly from the Caribbean. Wembley House School has long since gone, although the building remains and for many years has functioned as a community centre for Asian ladies.

Nonetheless, despite the changes that have occurred, I feel a pull to the place where I grew up, and enjoy cycling there once a year from the home Jillie and I retired to in Westminster in the centre of London. The people now living in Wembley are kind and, apart from certain cultural differences, are very similar to us. When she retired, Mum sold the shop and our home above it to a Mr Poppat, an Indian trader, whose family still run it. Richard and I have been in there on a couple of occasions and introduced ourselves to them, and on each occasion they have been very welcoming and interested to hear that we lived there a long time ago.

# ABOUT THE AUTHOR

**D**ouglas Model is a retired consultant physician. Before taking up medicine, he spent ten years as a navigating officer on large passenger and cargo ships running to Australasia and all over the world. He spent his childhood, aged 6 to 11, living in London during the war. His memoir *My Friend The Sea* has been well received on Amazon, and he has previously written articles for *The Guardian*, *The BMJ*, *The Lancet* and other journals. He lives in Westminster with his wife Jillie.

The destination for history
www.thehistorypress.co.uk